SHROPSHIRE PUB WALKS

Judy Smith

COUNTRYSIDE BOOKS
NEWBURY BERKSHIRE

Path in Comer Woods

First published 2023
© 2023 Judy Smith

All rights reserved. No part of this publication may be reproduced, stored in a retrieval system, or transmitted by any means, electronic, mechanical, photocopying, recording or otherwise, without the prior written permission of the copyright holder and publishers.

COUNTRYSIDE BOOKS
3 Catherine Road
Newbury, Berkshire, RG14 7NA

To view our complete range of books,
please visit us at
www.countrysidebooks.co.uk

ISBN 978 1 84674 418 1

All materials used in the manufacture of this book carry FSC certification

For Luca, our transatlantic grandson.
One day may you get to walk in Shropshire – and, of course,
to enjoy some real English pubs!

Produced through The Letterworks Ltd., Reading
Designed and Typeset by KT Designs, St Helens
Printed by Holywell Press, Oxford

CONTENTS

Introduction — 5
Area map — 6

WALK

1 Selattyn: The Docks (*3 miles / 5 km*) — 8
2 Welshampton: The Sun Inn (*3 miles / 4.8 km*) — 13
3 Ash Magna: The White Lion (*3½ miles / 5.6 km*) — 17
4 Loppington: The Dickin Arms (*4 miles / 6.4 km*) — 21
5 Pant: The Cross Guns (*5 miles / 8.2 km*) — 25
6 Nesscliffe: The Old Three Pigeons (*4¼ miles / 6.8 km*) — 30

7	Cheswardine: The Wharf Tavern (4½ miles / 7.2 km)	35
8	Edgmond: The Lamb Inn (5½ miles / 8.8 km)	39
9	Pontesbury: The Nag's Head (5 miles / 8 km)	44
10	Cound: The Riverside Inn (3½ miles / 5.5 km)	48
11	Kemberton: The Masons Arms (4 miles / 6.4 km)	53
12	Quatford: The Danery (5 miles / 8 km)	57
13	Much Wenlock: The Talbot (4½ miles / 7.4 km)	62
14	Picklescott: The Bottle and Glass (4 miles / 6.4 km)	66
15	Stiperstones: The Stiperstones Inn (4 miles / 6.6 km)	71
16	All Stretton: The Yew Tree (4½ miles / 7.2 km)	75
17	Clun: The White Horse Inn (6 miles / 9.8 km)	80
18	Aston Munslow: The Swan Inn (5½ miles / 8.8 km)	84
19	Ludlow: The Rose and Crown (6 miles / 9.7 km)	88
20	Hopton Wafers: The Hopton Crown (4½ miles / 7.2 km)	92

Brown Moss

INTRODUCTION

It's a fine frosty Sunday morning, the dog is looking longingly at his lead, and you feel you would like to go somewhere different today. Most particularly, your thoughts are turning to a short walk followed by a hearty pub lunch, and for just that, you will find here 20 suggestions. Of course it doesn't have to be Sunday, or a morning either – and you certainly don't need to have a dog, although with each walk and pub, I have indicated how suitable it might be for your four-footed friend. These are simply walks that for the most part can be completed in under three hours, giving you plenty of time to enjoy a pub meal afterwards if that is what you would like to do.

It is always a pleasure to walk in Shropshire. The county may not have the drama of some, the high mountains, cliffs or coastal expanses, but it has variety in spades! The walks here amble through the low-lying mosses and meres of the north and climb to the panoramic heights of Stiperstones and the Long Mynd; they wander through the woodland of the Severn and Clun valleys, and traverse the rich farmland around the River Teme in the south. And in and among all those walks are curious features you may never have known existed in Shropshire – a ring for bulls set in a village street, a highwayman's cave, a disused canal as lovely as a long lake, a waterfall, a barytes mine, a village pound, and more. Discovering these hidden gems adds spice to every walk.

The variation and interest in the landscape is surely matched by the same in the pubs. There are ancient hostelries here – one known to have served ale over seven centuries, one whose premises are mentioned in the Domesday Book, another that hosted Dick Turpin – and certainly black beams, log fires and cruck timbers are much in evidence. But along with those are sleek modern establishments, and pubs with large flower-filled beer gardens and children's playgrounds; there are pubs with a view of hills or a river, a community-run pub, and one

Area map showing locations of the walks

with its own wood-fired pizza oven. We have had a wonderful time visiting so many of Shropshire's pubs. The ones you find here are the 'pick of the bunch'! Do I have a favourite? Well, actually I do, but I'm not going to declare it. Visit them all and you could answer that question yourself.

While talking about the pubs, I should say that only the genre of the cuisine is mentioned because actual details of food served can change overnight. Suffice to say that in these pages are pubs whose menus are quite up-market, while others simply offer good hearty fare, with the accent on local produce, and Shropshire ales to accompany. Of course, all are hiker-friendly.

If you manage to take every walk in this book you will have covered almost 100 miles – and I'm not sure that you will have walked off all the calories consumed in those pubs! But more importantly perhaps, you will have savoured the rich diversity of Shropshire and had a glimpse of some of its more remote corners. I hope you enjoy it all as much as we did.

In conclusion, I really must thank my husband Eric for his support. His was the burden of sharing all those pub meals with me. A hard life!

And now get boots in the car, and off you go. Where will you walk first? Have fun on your travels!

Judy Smith

PUBLISHER'S NOTE

We hope that you obtain considerable enjoyment from this book; great care has been taken in its preparation. Although at the time of publication all routes followed public rights of way or permitted paths, diversion orders can be made and permissions withdrawn.

We cannot, of course, be held responsible for such diversion orders or any inaccuracies in the text which result from these or any other changes to the routes, nor any damage which might result from walkers trespassing on private property. We are anxious, though, that all the details covering the walks are kept up to date, and would therefore welcome information from readers which would be relevant to future editions.

The simple sketch maps that accompany the walks in this book are based on notes made by the author whilst surveying the routes on the ground. They are designed to show you how to reach the start and to point out the main features of the overall circuit, and they contain a progression of numbers that relate to the paragraphs of the text.

However, for the benefit of a proper map, we do recommend that you purchase the relevant Ordnance Survey sheet covering your walk. Ordnance Survey maps are widely available, especially through booksellers and local newsagents.

Walk 1
SELATTYN

Distance: 3 miles (5 km)

Start: The Docks, Glyn Road, Selattyn, SY10 7DH.

Parking: At The Docks with the permission of the proprietor, otherwise roadside in the village along Glyn Road (B4579).

Map: OS Explorer 240 Oswestry. **Grid Ref:** SJ266340.

Terrain: Field and woodland paths. Short stretch on a quiet B road. Track crossing the streams in Point 3 can be muddy after wet weather. Seven stiles.

When the forest and dense undergrowth were cleared on Selattyn Hill they found an old stone tower. Unfortunately there was no 'Sleeping Beauty' princess inside! But that tower was built in 1847 when the bare hilltop would have offered tremendous views, and it was intended as a memorial to a 6th-century prince who died in battle in the valley below. The tower actually stands

Selattyn 1

within a Bronze Age ring cairn which you can still see today as a circle of raised ground.

This walk takes you on an easy climb to Selattyn Tower, which is sadly becoming engulfed in vegetation again. But to appreciate the panorama it once enjoyed, you need only walk on a few metres to the woodland edge. Before your gaze, the Shropshire Plain merges into that of Cheshire, with the Shropshire Hills lifting the horizon to the right and the waters of the Mersey estuary glinting far on the other side. A bench encourages you to linger.

THE PUB

THE DOCKS seems a curious name for a hillside pub where the nearest water is many miles away! Originally called the Cross Keys, it seems the 'Docks' is a name that evolved locally, maybe as a place to do deals, maybe as a place to refuel. No-one really knows, but The Docks can certainly refuel you today, with an excellent range of wines, draught beers and real ales alongside a well-chosen menu. Add to that its character of tiny low-beamed rooms and log fires and you have a popular venue. It could be as well to book. Dog-friendly.
⊕ thedocksselattyn.co.uk ☎ 01691 653347.

The Walk

❶ With **The Docks** behind you, turn right along the village road in the direction of **Craignant**, and at the U-bend in about 400 metres, go left on a signed footpath into woodland. After two close stiles, there's a less-than-obvious right then left kink in the path, beyond which it continues clearly, climbing through the woods.

❷ Reaching a kissing gate at the woodland edge, bear half right across the field, along the line of the dip. A stile at the top right now allows you to leave the field, and a stile a few metres farther on gives access to another. Keep to the woodland edge initially, but eventually aim for a metal gate in the top right corner, beyond which a third field rises to a house. Cross the field to a gateway below the house, on the left.

❸ Through the gateway, turn left to descend the field and cross a

Shropshire Pub Walks

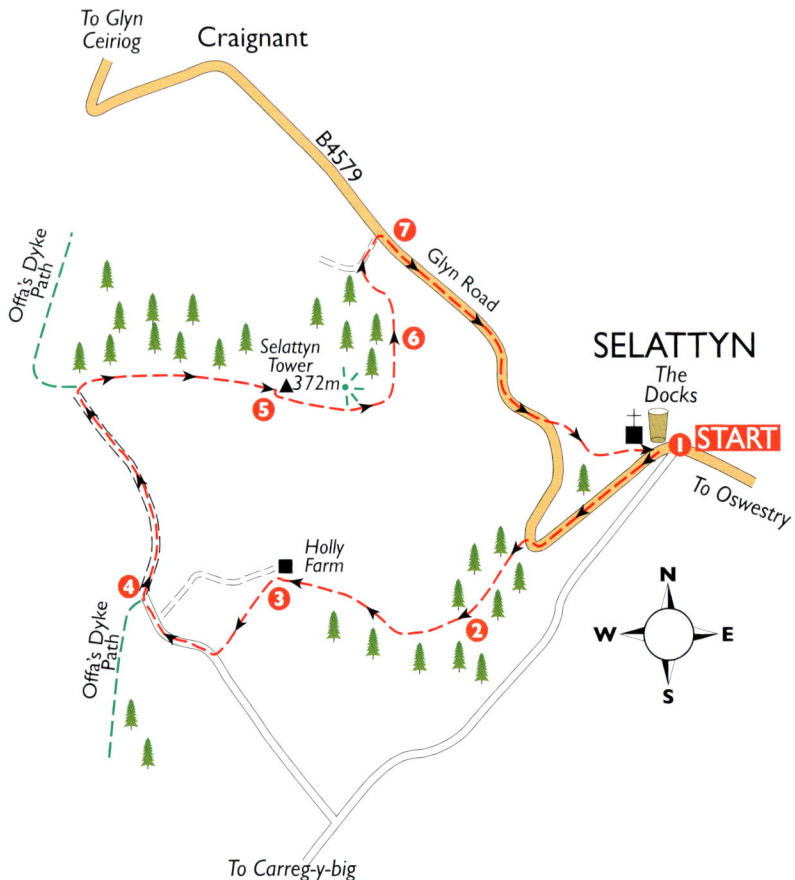

stream on a track that can be muddy. Keep right of the fence, rising and descending to cross a second stream. Maintaining the direction on the far side quickly brings you to a metal gate into a lane. Turn right here, and continue uphill for some 400 metres to a path junction.

4 Turn right, now on the signed **Offa's Dyke Path**, and climb gently up **Selattyn Hill**. Beside a waymarked post at the top, turn right and walk through the rough field with the woodland edge immediately on your left. Continue into the fenced corner, where a stile beside a gate gives access to the wood. Go right, then

Selattyn 1

immediately branch left on a narrow path under the conifers. Quite quickly you reach the grey ruins of **Selattyn Tower**.

5 Passing the tower on your left, walk downhill and cross another track to the seat with its fine view at the woodland edge. Go through the kissing gate here and walk downhill to a stile at the bottom left corner of the field. Continue descending, going through a kissing gate near a ruined building, and carrying on downhill. At the bottom of this field, turn sharp left, and with a wall on your right, walk towards the wood.

6 A kissing gate takes you through to a path skirting the lower edge of the wood. Eventually reaching a concrete track, turn right to descend sharply and meet the **B4579**.

7 Go right now, and follow this quiet road for some 700 metres to the outskirts of Selattyn. With a brick house on your left, go over a stile on the left and descend the field, bearing right at the bottom. Here a wooden footbridge vaults the stream and the

Shropshire Pub Walks

uphill path beyond soon returns you to the church and inn at Selattyn.

Place of Interest Nearby

Some 2 miles to the north, **Chirk Castle**, now in the care of the National Trust, was built around 1300 as part of Edward I's defence of the Welsh Marches. After many changes of hands, in 1595 it came into the possession of the Myddelton family who have lived in it continuously since that time. Today its various rooms reflect the changing fashions and tastes of its occupants over four centuries, while the extensive estate and landscaped gardens offer some excellent walks. Sat Nav LL14 5AF.
⊕ nationaltrust.org.uk/chirk-castle.

Walk 2
WELSHAMPTON

Distance: 3 miles (4.8 km)

Start: The Sun Inn, A495, Welshampton, SY12 0PH.

Parking: At the Sun Inn for patrons, or alternatively, there is a car park behind the school, about 300 metres further along the A495 towards Ellesmere.

Map: OS Explorer 241 Shrewsbury. **Grid Ref:** SJ436350.

Terrain: Quiet lanes, canal towpath and field paths. No stiles, dog-friendly.

This northern corner of Shropshire is a timeless land, a place of low-lying fields and patchy woodland, winding high-banked lanes and scattered brick farms. Through this gentle scenery flows the Llangollen Canal – and indeed, unlike other canals, it does have a flow, being fed by the rushing River Dee at its source. This walk takes you down along the banks of that canal, and here you may expect to see some action, since among leisure boaters, the Llangollen is the country's most popular waterway. The return

Shropshire Pub Walks

along a lonely lane and a bridleway between open fields may seem quite peaceful in contrast!

THE PUB — **THE SUN INN** certainly doesn't look like a cottage from the outside, but step through the door into the bar and all the atmosphere is there - low ceilings, two log fires, log-stack on the wall, bare wooden tables, low seating, plants, books, a mantel clock, all the feeling of home-from-home, and a great place to relax. But should you want more formal dining, there are also attractive small rooms set aside for just that. With a cheerful beer garden, a menu that uses local produce whenever possible, and real ales and cider on tap, The Sun Inn is both friendly and dog-friendly.
⊕ thesuninn.net ☎ 01948 710847.

The Walk

❶ With the **Sun Inn** behind you, turn right along the main road to cross it in front of the church.
The Church of St Michael and All Angels was designed by Gilbert Scott, and interestingly, has a jacquard patterned roof. Its grounds contain the grave of a prince of Lesotho, who while

Welshampton 2

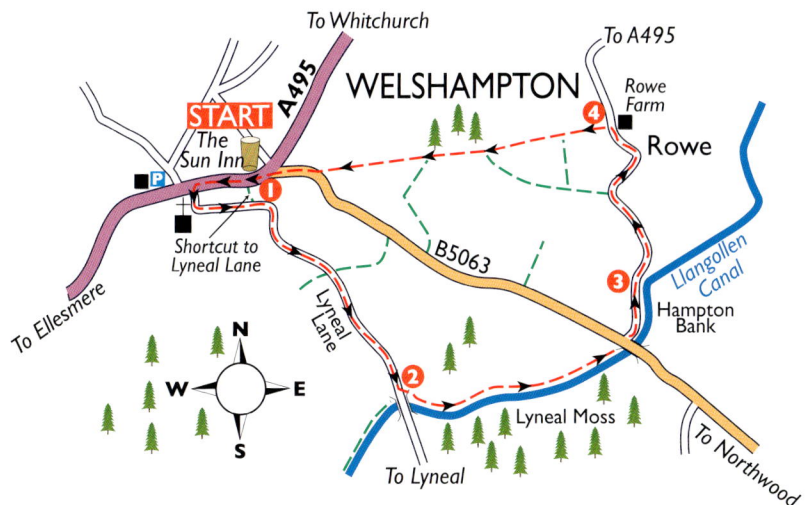

studying to be a priest, visited the church at its consecration in 1863, and catching a 'fever', died there. In 2010, the Queen of Lesotho visited his grave.

Continue with the walk by turning down **Lyneal Lane**, running alongside the churchyard, and carry on for about a mile to reach a bridge over the canal.

(If you are starting from **The Sun car park**, an inconspicuously-signed footpath opposite the car park offers a short cut to **Lyneal Lane**.)

❷ Steps just before the bridge lead down to the canal towpath. Turn left along it (canal on your right) and enjoy the watery scene for something like another mile to arrive at a brick bridge, **Bridge 50**. Go under this and continue for another 200m, to where a small gate allows you access to a minor road alongside.

❸ Turn right on the road, and quite soon you begin to encounter the scattered houses that make up the hamlet of **Rowe**. Ignore the first footpath signed off on the left.

❹ Opposite brick-built **Rowe Farm**, go through a large metal gate on to an open grassy track between two fields. The track is not

Shropshire Pub Walks

Ellesmere

signed off the road, but once on it, a sign on a telegraph pole confirms that it is a bridleway. Climb gently uphill towards a spinney on the horizon, alongside which the track becomes hedged briefly. Beyond the spinney the obvious track runs alongside a field and then becomes the long drive of a house to arrive at a road. Turn right to quickly reach the main road. **The Sun Inn** is directly ahead here, and the church and village car park are just a couple of minutes' walk to your left.

Place of Interest Nearby

A couple of miles to the west, the market town of Ellesmere is peppered with black-and-white half-timbered buildings and elegant Georgian houses. Once a canal centre (an arm of water runs right up into the town), its main attraction today is 'The Mere', a huge lake on its outskirts. The scene here seems to have changed little since the 1930s, when the then owner, Lord Brownlow, built a boathouse beside the water. The grand Wellingtonias and abundant rhododendrons of adjacent Cremorne Gardens were all part of Lord Brownlow's estate, which was generously given to the public in 1953. Today you can enjoy a very pleasant lakeside walk, or maybe take out a rowing boat on the water. Sat Nav SY12 0PA.

Walk 3
Ash Magna

Distance: 3½ miles (5.6km)

Start: The White Lion, Church Lane, Ash Magna, Whitchurch, SY13 4DR.

Parking: At the White Lion with permission from the manager, or in the large car park behind the adjacent village hall.

Map: OS Explorer 241 Shrewsbury. **Grid Ref:** SJ572397.

Terrain: Field and woodland paths. An almost level walk. 2 stiles.

North Shropshire is the land of 'Mosses and Meres' – meres being pools of water from retreating Ice Age glaciers trapped in hollows of the land, and mosses, peat bogs created over time as decaying vegetation filled up the meres. The walk here takes you across low-lying fields to Brown Moss, a wetland area that is

Shropshire Pub Walks

now a Local Nature Reserve and Site of Special Scientific Interest. The path leads through woods and reed beds, and around a big central lake where the rare floating water-plantain can be found. Other unusual plants abound, as do frogs, newts, dragonflies and a variety of bird life. It all makes a fascinating short walk, but don't forget the waterproof footwear!

THE PUB

THE WHITE LION is an attractive pub in an attractive village, and has been owned by the local community since 2017. The interior is classic village hostelry – beams, log fires, wooden tables, beer mirrors on the walls. Nothing in its rustic simplicity prepares you for the quality of the food, which is locally sourced and truly of a very high standard. You can enjoy it beside a blazing fire in winter or out in the little wild flower beer garden in summer.

And don't hesitate to bring your dog along, too. He may even be welcomed with a treat!
⊕ whitelionash.co.uk ☎ 01948 663153.

The Walk

❶ Leaving the car park or the pub, turn left in the direction of **Ightfield**. There's now a pavement, and later a path set back from the road, to take you to the village of **Ash Parva**. At the crossroads here, turn right down **Ash Lane** and continue for about a mile to a signed footpath, immediately before some cottages on the right.

❷ Take the footpath, going alongside a cottage and then past stables, to a stile beside a gate leading on to another lane. Go left here, and in about 50 metres, take another signed path on the right. This now crosses a field to its top right-hand corner where a kissing gate hiding in a hedge admits you to a second field. Bend left then right around a thicket, then leave the field at the far right corner on a short path through woodland.

Ash Magna 3

3 At the lane here turn right, and after about 500 metres, reach a sign telling you that you have arrived at the reserve of **Brown Moss**. Continue ahead, ignoring the first track on the left to reach a signed path through a wooden kissing gate on the same side. Now simply keep ahead as signed on the **Shropshire Way**, always with the mere through trees on your right.

4 With the white, half-timbered **Beehive Cottage** ahead, go through a kissing gate to leave the reserve and immediately bear right to re-enter it. The main path takes you on, soon going through a potentially muddy patch through reed beds, to reach a junction on the far side. Turn right here on a path that soon bends right to cross the swamp on a wooden bridge, and finally leads you to an open grassy space with a seat ahead.

5 Bear left towards a car park in the trees, but keep right of it, going beside the mere. Keep on the mereside path, passing a bench, and

19

Shropshire Pub Walks

then a kissing gate on the left. Go through a second kissing gate and cross the lane to the wide track opposite. Before reaching a metal gate, a narrow path winds off into trees on the right. Go with it to reach a track junction.

6 Turn left here, and soon go through a small gate to continue alongside a field. A gate admits you to a second field where a clear path climbs uphill towards the houses. At its exit on to a lane turn left, then in a few metres go right on the main road through the village to return to the car park and pub.

Place of Interest Nearby

Do you fancy a little wild water swimming? Or maybe a lesson in paddle-boarding? Watery Brown Moss, passed on the walk, certainly isn't the place for such but just up the road (near the A41/B5476 roundabout), **Alderford Lake** can offer that and a lot more. Owned by an enterprising local family, the restaurant, farm shop, woodland walks, canoes, aquabikes, climbing wall and all the rest, make this a popular (though not without cost) family destination. Sat Nav SY13 3JQ. ⊕ alderford.com

Nook Farm

Walk 4
LOPPINGTON

Distance: 4 miles (6.4 km)

Start: The Dickin Arms, Loppington, SY4 5SR.

Parking: At the Dickin Arms for patrons. Otherwise, there is free parking behind the village hall, some 50 metres north-east along the main village road.

Map: OS Explorer 241 Shrewsbury. **Grid Ref:** SJ470293.

Terrain: Field paths, quiet lanes. Many stiles.

You could easily spend the whole morning in Loppington and never get out for a walk at all! The village has so many listed buildings, most of which are timber-framed and painted in tasteful colours. Along the main street you can look out for tiny Cruck Cottage, its roof supported by classic Shropshire leaning arch beams, Rowan Cottage, once the Blacksmith's Arms, and early 18th-century Loppington Hall among others. Nook Farm, passed on the walk, is another gem. Then there are the curiosities – the bull ring in the road outside the Dickin Arms, once used

Shropshire Pub Walks

for bull baiting, the 17th-century sundial in the churchyard, the old village pump beside the village hall and the village pound. When you can tear yourself away, this walk takes you to the highest and lowest points in the area – not that there's much difference between them. A windmill once stood on the ridge rising to 103 metres, while some 10 metres below, Brownheath Moss is a Site of Special Scientific Interest. And between is a gently rolling landscape of fields, woods, and farms, unchanged over centuries.

THE PUB **THE DICKIN ARMS**, named after local gentry, has been serving ales in the village of Loppington for something approaching 200 years, although the building itself is much older than that. Inside it has been sympathetically and stylishly restored, with oak beams, oak tables and flag floors – and in the bar at least, more than a nod to country pursuits with pheasants, partridges, foxes  and owls adorning the walls in various guises. The excellent locally-sourced food is artistically served in both restaurant and bar, with a good range of ales and wines, and even 'signature cocktails'. Canine guests can claim their own refreshment from the jar on the counter!
🌐 thedickinarms.co.uk ☎ 01939 233471.

The Walk

❶ On the **Main Street**, with the **Dickin Arms** behind you, go right to find a stile leading into a very narrow hedged footpath immediately after **Parish Farm**. Over a stile at its end, bear diagonally right to another stile near the top right-hand corner of the field. In the next field, keep left of the hedge, and do the same in the next field to arrive at a lane.

❷ Turn right on the lane. After about 600 metres, just before **Mill Cottage**, take a path signed on the left. This now climbs gently alongside the hedge to bring you out at **Mill House**, once the site

Loppington 4

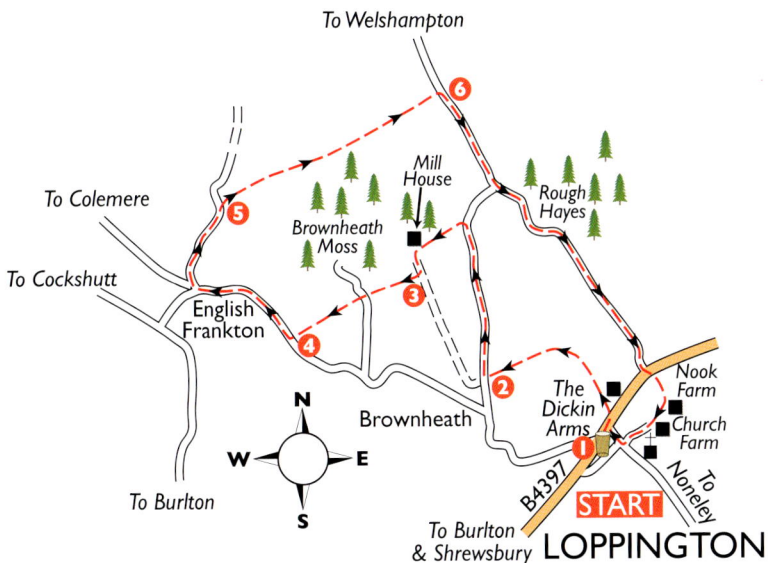

of a windmill. Turn left on its drive, and after some 30 metres, right over a stile in the hedge.

3 Aim now to the left of a small cottage at the lower edge of the field to find yet another stile. Cross the lane here directly to a path between high hedges. The path now runs just right of the hedge through two more fields to emerge on a lane.

4 Turn right on the lane and walk up to the junction at **English Frankton**. Bear right here as signed to **Colemere**, and then right again on a No Through Road. After about 300 metres the road bends left and you reach a kissing gate in the hedge on the right.

5 Through the kissing gate, aim diagonally left in the field to a stile in its top left corner. In the next fields, divided by a wooden fence, keep the hedge on your left to reach a bridge over a ditch leading into the next field.
To the right here, the wooded area is Brownheath Moss. The ditch is draining its boggy depths.
The path now maintains the same direction, crossing the narrow

end of the field to a stile in the hedge opposite. Keep left of the tree-fringed pond ahead and climb the ridge (as high as Mill House) on a path to the right of the hedge. A gap in the hedge admits you to a final field. Bear right along the line of the telegraph poles to a stile on the bank above the lane.

6 Go right on the lane, ignore the only right turning, and continue past the woodland of **Rough Hayes** to the main road on the outskirts of **Loppington**. Cross the road directly to a stile opposite and bear diagonally right towards the house on the far side. A stile now gives access to a lane where you turn right.

To your left is handsome, half-timbered Nook Farm, and beyond it, Church Farm, its building dating from the 17th century. Farther on, Old Pound Cottage has the former pound at its doors, and the Church of St Michael and All Angels opposite has features from Norman times.

Turn right at the church for the **Dickin Arms**, and right again on the main road to return to the **Village Hall**.

Place of Interest Nearby

You had just a glimpse of **Brownheath Moss** on this walk, but some 4 miles to the north is **Whixall Moss**, which together with adjacent **Bettisfield Moss** and **Fenn's Moss** forms one of the largest peat bogs in this country. Whixall Moss is vast, and atmospheric to say the least, its low lying cotton-sedge-filled ground scattered with ponds created by former peat diggings. Rare wildlife abounds, from insects, spiders, dragonflies and butterflies to curlews, lizards, and adders. Signed walking trails have been created across the Moss, and leaflets at its entrance (Morris's Bridge, SY13 2RT) offer some background. It's very different, and worth taking a look.

Walk 5
Pant

Distance: 5 miles (8.2 km)

Start: The Cross Guns, Rockwell Lane, Pant, SY10 9QR.

Parking: At the Cross Guns by permission of the proprietor or on nearby roadsides.

Map: OS Explorer 240 Oswestry. **Grid Ref:** SJ273220.

Terrain: Woodland paths, canal towpath. Uneven descent of Llanymynech Hill. No stiles. Dog-friendly.

Certainly this begins as a 'Walk in the Woods', but then there are so many added extras! Llynclys Common Nature Reserve, a veritable leafy wilderness with an abundance of wild flowers and butterflies, is followed by a long descent of Llanymynech Hill, with tremendous views south-west into mid-Wales. Farther on still, you'll want to linger in Llanymynech Heritage Area, where limestone from quarries on the hill was fired in a huge Hoffmann Kiln to produce lime for agricultural fertiliser and mortar for building. The lime was transported along the Montgomery

Shropshire Pub Walks

Canal, and the way back lies along the towpath of a dry section of this old waterway.

THE CROSS GUNS is a friendly pub with a large garden, good value meals, and cask ales on tap. Why the name Cross Guns? Well, cross-guns is the badge of an army marksman and it seems there was once a rifle range nearby. There's not a gun in sight today though, just some low seating beside an open log fire and a long dining area with outside views. The open but divided nature of the whole facilitates a quick game of pool while waiting for your meal and is also dog-friendly.
🌐 facebook.com/CrossGunsPant   ☎ 01691 839631.

The Walk

1 Leave the **Cross Guns** walking uphill on **Briggs Lane**, and at the crossroads at the top, keep ahead on **Tregarthen Lane**. Continue climbing for around 400 metres to find a footpath sign on the right, and just a few metres beyond it, a hard-surfaced bridleway on the same side, heading into woods. After ½ mile or so on this bridleway you emerge at a junction beside houses. Bear right here and continue on the bridleway to a junction with a signboard at a sharp right-hand bend.

Pant 5

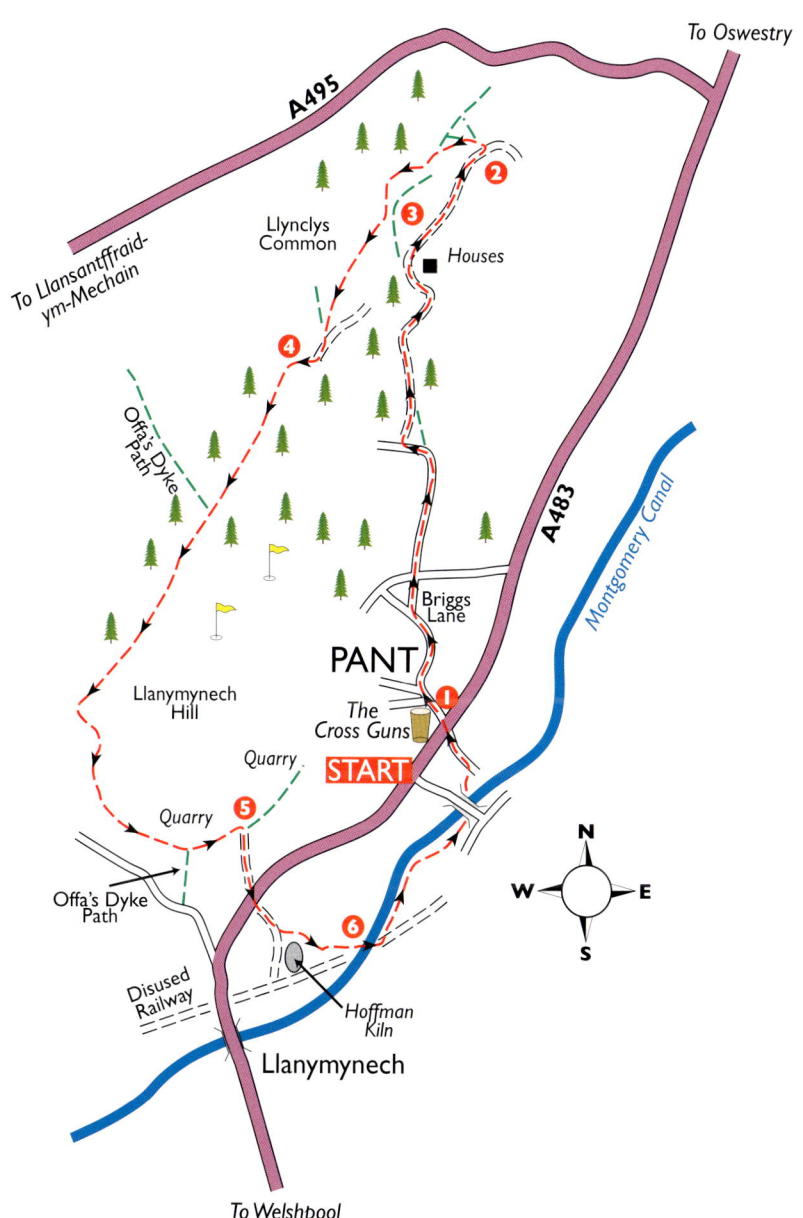

27

Shropshire Pub Walks

② Here take the second path on the left, the wider of the two, heading into the woods. At a fork a few metres in, bear left, and at a second fork soon afterwards, bear left again to arrive at a track junction. Left again here, uphill, and after the path narrows, left once more to go through a kissing gate on to **Llynclys Common**. The path ahead now climbs to a grassy plateau with a large silver birch tree as centrepiece.

③ Turn right at the tree and walk down the wide ride, soon picking up **Shropshire Way** signs, and passing through a wooden gateway. The main path climbs gently, and at length delivers you to another wooden gate with an area of clearance beyond. Keep ahead, bear left on a wider track, then right on a hard-surfaced track to reach a junction with a display board beside a house.

④ Turn right, passing the house to go left up steep steps beyond. You are now walking beside a sheer fenced edge. After about ½ mile, in a gully, the **Offa's Dyke Path** joins you from the right. Follow it along the edge of the golf course, then through a gate on the right to descend **Llanymynech Hill**, with far-reaching views, including the tall chimney of the **Hoffman Kiln**. After a quarry entrance on the left, keep ahead where the **Offa's Dyke Path** leaves, and continue to a junction with a winding wheel.

⑤ Turn right here going down the steep slope where once limestone-loaded trucks descended on rails. The path swings left at the bottom to duck under the road and enter the heritage area, with the building where the stone was once weighed on your left. Keep on the main path, then turn left where directed to the '**Hoffmann Kiln avoiding steps**'. Two tracks now lead to the huge furnace. Taking the upper one, you can have a good look around the kiln before continuing through a metal gate on its left side. At the next junction, go left on a narrow hard-surfaced track running along the edge of a meadow.

⑥ Reaching duckboards, turn right up steps, then down to cross the canal. To your right the canal is in water; to your left it is dry.
The Montgomery Canal became less important as Portland cement took over the role of lime mortar, and after a breach in

Pant 5

1936, it was abandoned. Today it is gradually being restored to accommodate holiday boaters.

Turn left on the towpath and follow it to the next bridge. Find a gate beyond the bridge and turn right to cross over it. In front of you now are old limekilns. Take the path running in front of them, then up steep steps alongside. Emerging on a track, continue ahead a few metres to a junction, and turn left on the lane. Just over the rise you reach the main road, and on its far side, the **Cross Guns**.

Place of Interest Nearby

Some four miles south-east of Pant is the village of **Melverley** with its remarkable church. Built of local oak, wattle and daub, and pegged together rather than nailed, the 'zebra-striped' edifice has survived the ravages of six centuries. The church houses a Saxon font, along with a Jacobean altar, pulpit, and decidedly tipsy balcony, and is always open. Sat Nav SY10 8PJ.

Walk 6
NESSCLIFFE

Distance: 4¼ miles (6.8 km)

Start: The Old Three Pigeons, Nesscliffe, SY4 1DB.

Parking: At the Old Three Pigeons for patrons. Otherwise, take the Valeswood road opposite and find The Oaks roadside parking, ½ mile on the right (and start the walk from Point 9). Sat Nav SY4 1DG.

Map: OS Explorers 240 Oswestry and 241 Shrewsbury.
Grid Ref: SJ382194.

Terrain: Field and woodland paths in gently rolling countryside. 2 stiles.

Here you are in highwayman territory. Humphrey Kynaston (d. 1534) was something of a Robin Hood character, robbing wealthy merchants returning from London along the old London road and distributing his spoils to the village poor. He and his

Nesscliffe 6

horse hid from the authorities in a two-room cave on Nesscliffe Hill, which you can see (but not go in) on this walk. Beyond is a badger sett, a village pump and pound, a high viewpoint, the ramparts of an Iron Age hillfort, open countryside and mixed woodland, making this a perfect before-a-hearty-lunch ramble.

THE PUB **THE OLD THREE PIGEONS**, dating from 1405, has a decor of oak beams and heavy wooden tables that respects its heritage, while the food represents the 21st century at its best. The inn is also dog-friendly and cosy, with an interesting choice of dining rooms. Surely there's no other pub that keeps a fireside seat for a highwayman – or at least his ghost! Truly, there are customers who swear they've met a spectre perched in that inglenook! ⊕ 3pigeons.co.uk ☎ 01743 741279.

The Walk

1 From the pub, cross to the road opposite and take a track on the right, signed to **Kynaston's Cave** and heading into woods. Meeting a broad cross-track, turn right and continue along the foot of the hill. Soon a path doubling-back left uphill is signed to Kynaston's Cave. It's worth taking a short diversion to see it before returning to the signpost and continuing along the lower track. Beyond a quarry and badger sett, a gate leads into a lane.

2 Here take the footpath opposite, running alongside the hedge, then bearing right across a field. Over a stile, keep right to skirt a pond, then bear left to a stile in the hedge opposite. After bearing right to traverse another short field you reach a barrier and gravelled track accessing a lane.

3 Turn right to enter the village of **Great Ness**. On your left now are the remains of the village pump, used until 1945, and almost opposite, the track up to the church was part of the old Holyhead coaching road. Continuing along the road, the village pound comes before two footpaths leaving on the left.

4 Go through a kissing gate to take the second of these paths, alongside a hedge. Three fields are now crossed keeping the

Nesscliffe

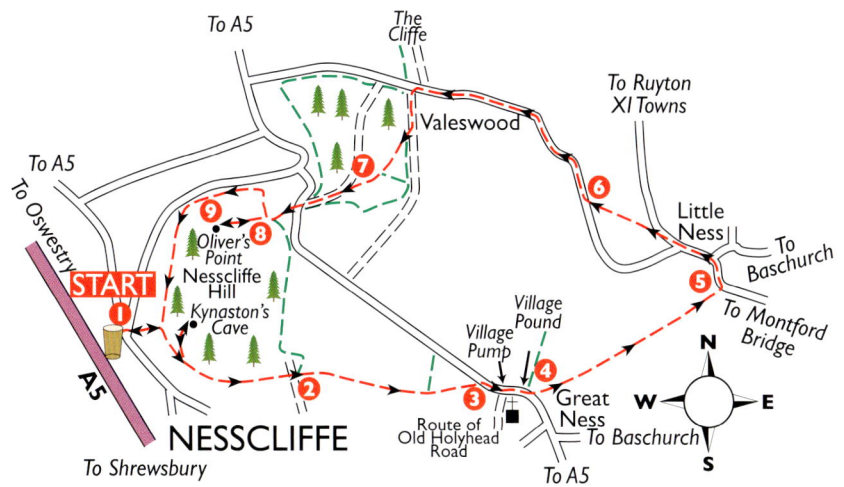

hedge on your left, before a high-hedged track takes you to meet a road at **Little Ness**.

5 Turn left, keep ahead at the first junction, and about 150 metres afterwards, go right at the second (**SP Ruyton**). Some 50 metres along, a small gate on the left admits you to a path bearing right across a huge field to a gate on the far side.

6 Turn right on the road here and continue into the ribbon village of **Valeswood**, with its interesting old and new houses. Pass a sign to **The Cliffe** on your right, and some 100 metres beyond, take a track on the left beside houses. Past the houses, paths enter the woodland on your right. Take the footpath (not the bridleway) bearing ahead right, and weave through the trees, always keeping right, to emerge at a wide hard-surfaced track.

7 Turn left here and soon pass **The Pines car park**. Cross the road beyond to a kissing gate, and continue alongside a field. Through a gate at the top, turn right to reach a fingerpost at a path junction.

8 Ahead now, the track leads through the ramparts of an Iron Age hillfort to **Oliver's Point** with its fine views. Go that way if you

Shropshire Pub Walks

will, but then return to the fingerpost to continue downhill, signed to **The Oaks Car Park**. The path bends left at the bottom, then passes the parking area on the right.

9 To return to the pub, continue above the parking area, bearing left at the path junction in some 200 metres. The path contours the lower edge of the wood, and in around ½ mile descends steep wooden steps. Turn right here to get back to the pub.

Place of Interest Nearby

The **British Ironwork Centre**, 6 miles north-west along the A5, offers a fascinating day out. The sculpture park features huge iron giraffes and elephants – a whole African safari – but there's much more, with the Knife Angel and Gorilla Apocalypse as the stars. Add to that an indoor exhibition, an excellent café, and retro ironwork from toys to kitchenware on sale. Open every day except Monday and Tuesday. Sat Nav SY11 4JH.
⊕ britishironworkcentre.co.uk

Walk 7
CHESWARDINE

Distance: 4½ miles (7.2 km)

Start: Wharf Tavern, Market Drayton, Goldstone, TF9 2LP.

Parking: At the Wharf Tavern with the permission of the proprietor. Otherwise start the walk from the Parish Hall in Cheswardine (Point 2). Sat Nav TF9 2RS.

Map: OS Explorer 243 Market Drayton. **Grid Ref:** SJ705295.

Terrain: Field and woodland paths, canal towpath, quiet lanes. Several stiles.

You could be forgiven for thinking that the Shropshire Union Canal would flow right through the heart of Shropshire. Not a bit of it! Instead it nips through a mere 10 miles or so in the far north-east corner of its eponymous county, spending most of its life in Staffordshire and Cheshire instead. This walk takes in just a short section of that canal, with a pub set right on its banks. It's an amble for a fine day in spring or summer, when the field paths are dry underfoot, the woodlands are bursting with bluebells and other wild flowers, and the canal is busy with colourful boats. This part of Shropshire is undulating agricultural

Shropshire Pub Walks

land for the most part, but is nonetheless attractive for that, and here around Cheswardine you have the very best of it.

THE PUB **THE WHARF TAVERN** is set on a site where coal was once transhipped and sold. Today the Wharf's smooth lawns stretch down to the water's edge and on a bright sunny day, there's nothing more relaxing than sitting at an outside table watching swans  dabbling in the shallows while brightly-painted narrowboats chug by. Should the weather be inclement, you have the same view from the window of the big dining room and a log-burner to keep you warm – but sadly your four-footed companion will not be allowed inside. The Wharf's widely-acclaimed menu is served lunchtime and evening every day.
⊕ wharfcaravanpark.co.uk/wharf-tavern ☎ 01630 661226.

The Walk

❶ Leaving the **Wharf Tavern**, cross the canal bridge and go through a gate on the left to join the towpath (canal on your left). Pass under the first bridge, and at the second (**Bridge 53**), go up steps to join the road and turn left. After some 400 metres of gentle climbing, a footpath sign points across a field on the left. Follow it diagonally right to cross a stile and continue to the right of a hedge. A small gate admits you to a hedged track, emerging at the playing field and **Parish Hall** of Cheswardine.

❷ Continue past the **Parish Hall** to the **High Street**, and turn left, uphill. After passing handsome **St Swithun's Church**, go right on Lawn Lane, which soon becomes a restricted byway running beside woodland. Where that woodland ends, the path forks. Bear left, crossing between fields to descend to a stile before more woods that bear the name **Lawn Drumble**.

> *A 'drumble' seems to be a local term for woodland. Lawn Drumble is carpeted with wood anemones, wild garlic, and bluebells, a feast for the eyes in springtime.*

Cheswardine 7

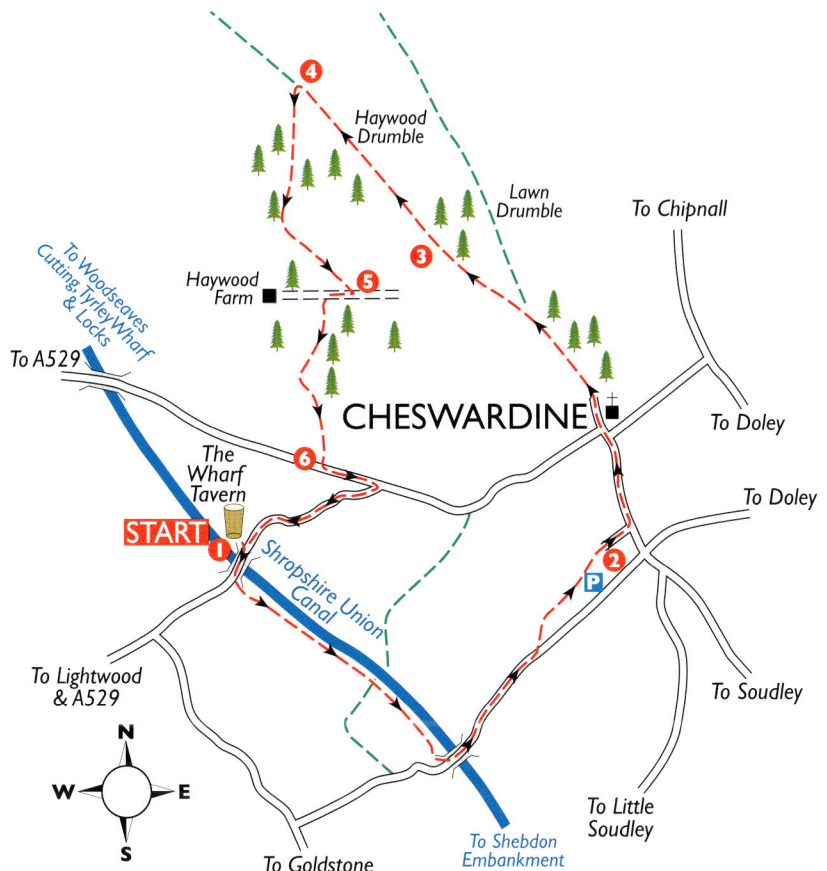

❸ The path crosses a stream and winds on through the wood to emerge at a field. Keep right of the hedge as signed, and continue to the next woodland, **Haywood Drumble**. Pass between two ponds here, then wind around a third to reach a stile into a large field. The path now runs left of the hedge to the top field corner.

❹ Turn very sharp left and walk diagonally across the middle of the field you have just skirted, aiming for a slight dip in the tree line ahead. Here a stile admits you to a path cutting briefly back through **Haywood Drumble**. With a large field ahead, aim for the buildings of **Haywood Farm** to reach a projecting field corner.

Shropshire Pub Walks

> *The path from here has been re-routed, and is not as shown on the OS map, but the new route is well waymarked.*

Now keep ahead with the hedge on your right, and continue past woodland. Go through a gap into a field and soon find a large gap on the right giving access to a farm track.

5 Turn right on the track, and in about 40 metres, go left on a footpath running alongside woodland with a stream in its depths. Continue to the far field corner, where a stile takes you into the wood. Ignore a path left crossing the stream, and keep ahead to go through a gap into a field. The path now leads on between crops to reach a road.

6 Turn left on the road, and in some 250 metres, take a road on the right. After descending gradually for some 700 metres, you arrive at the **Wharf Tavern**.

Place of Interest Nearby

Canal heritage is rich around Cheswardine. This part of the Shropshire Union was constructed in the early 1800s, when the aim was to avoid locks whenever possible. To the south of Cheswardine, a high embankment was built, while to the north is the 100 ft deep thickly-wooded, **Woodseaves Cutting**. Boats traversing its damp greenery say it has an 'African Queen' effect. If you fancy walking that way, don't even think it. The towpath can be as overgrown as the waterway, with the added ingredient of mud.

But beyond Woodseaves is **Tyrley Wharf**, from where five finally-needed locks cut deeply into the sandstone to take the canal down to Market Drayton's level. It's worth driving round to watch the efforts of the boaters in these locks with their difficult side-streams. Sat Nav TF9 2AH.

Walk 8
Edgmond

Distance: 5½ miles (8.8 km)

Start: The Lamb Inn, Shrewsbury Road, Edgmond, TF10 8HU.

Parking: At The Lamb Inn for patrons. Otherwise, there is free parking at the playing field 200 metres down the road into the village.

Map: OS Explorers 242 Telford and 243 Market Drayton.
Grid Ref: SJ723200.

Terrain: Field paths, quiet lanes, canal towpath. Dog friendly.

Once upon a time there was a canal passing through Edgmond, with narrowboats carrying, for the most part, coal for the town of Shrewsbury. Known as the Shrewsbury and Newport Canal, it connected to the rest of Britain's extensive canal system just a few miles to the east. Inevitably its use declined with the advent of the railways and, like so many other canals, it was abandoned by the Act of Parliament in 1944. Happily though, the mile and a half

Shropshire Pub Walks

between Edgmond and Newport have remained in water. That short section forms the focus of this walk and it is so peaceful in an urban area. Mallards dabble, swans nest, and dragonflies hover above drifting water lilies and reed-fringed banks. At one point there is an obvious former toll house: elsewhere old lock chambers are filled with flowering water weeds. There are plans afoot to restore this waterway for use by leisure boaters, but can it ever be as attractive as it is now? From Newport, it's an easy return across fields and around the edge of Chetwynd Deer Park. There's a fine lake to admire but don't expect to spot any deer!

THE PUB **THE LAMB INN**, although rather austere on the outside, gives a very different impression once inside. All is space and light, modern decor, high beams, and a curious round glass drinks display to greet you at the door. The Lamb is dog-friendly and family-friendly, with inviting outdoor seating, and a large beer garden with a playground. On offer is a good selection of beers and ales, and a wide menu.
🌐 thelambedgmond.co.uk ☎ 01952 879829.

Edgmond 8

The Walk

1 From The **Lamb Inn car park**, turn right on the road running alongside the pub (**Shrewsbury Road**) and walk into the village, passing the playing field with its parking area. At the junction with **High Street**, cross straight over into **Newport Road** and when this road bends sharp left, keep ahead on a signed track, lined with cherry trees. The track corners left, and where it ends, a kissing gate gives access to a narrow track between fences. Following this to its end, you emerge on the banks of the **Newport Canal**, at a site that was once **Polly's Lock**.

2 At this point you can choose to follow the gravelled towpath on the right or the lesser waterside track on the left. If you take the latter, you will need to cross over on the footbridge beside the next lock, known as **Tickethouse**. Boatmen travelling the canal needed to collect tickets to present to their masters for payment. The ticketmaster's toll house still stands beside the canal. Continue now on the towpath to reach the road bridge at **Town Lock**.

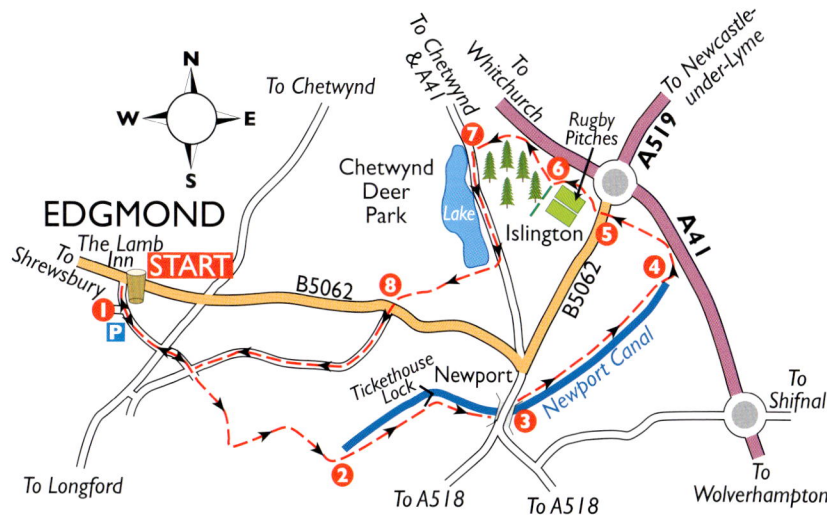

41

Shropshire Pub Walks

❸ Crouch low to pass under the bridge and cross to the towpath, which is now left of the canal. The lovely rural scene continues for a further ¾ mile, where the canal ends.

❹ Go left at the path junction here, on a path that climbs to run parallel to but above the busy **A41**. After some 100 metres the path bends away and soon becomes a tarmacked lane.

❺ At its end, cross over the road diagonally left to take a path into the playing fields. The path bends right around the garden of a house, then at its end, turns left to run alongside the first rugby pitch. Where it ends, bear slightly right to the edge of the nearby woodland, and follow it briefly to find a metal kissing gate on your right.

❻ Through this, the path contours the hill to reach more woodland. Go left through the trees or right along the field below here –

Edgmond 8

both arrive at the same place at the edge of the wood. From this point, cross the field, bearing left at its end to arrive at a road with a red sandstone wall on the far side.

7 Over the wall is a huge lake in **Chetwynd Deer Park**. Unless you are very tall, you won't be able to see it, but turn left on the pavement, and at the bottom of the hill the wall is lower. Continue to the wall's end, passing the lodge (view through the gates), and a few metres further on, turn through a kissing gate on the right. The path runs along the boundary of the park to meet a road.

8 Cross diagonally left to signed **Newport Road**. Keep to this for almost a mile to return to the corner you passed in Point 1. Turn right with the road, and retrace your steps to the Lamb Inn.

Place of Interest Nearby

Some three miles south of Edgmond are the ruins of **Lilleshall Abbey**, founded in Norman times, and belonging to the austere Arrouaisian order of Augustinians. Decommissioned after the Dissolution, it was partly destroyed by the Parliamentarians. Remaining today are the walls of the 12th-century abbey church, alongside cloisters and a processional door with some fine carving. It is an evocative site – and you could spot the black-robed ghostly monk who apparently drifts by from time to time! The Abbey is under the care of English Heritage and the site is freely accessible 10am to 6pm in summer, 10am to 4pm in winter.
Sat Nav TF10 9HW.
⊕ english-heritage.org.uk/visit/places/lilleshall-abbey

Walk 9

PONTESBURY

Distance: 5 miles (8 km)

Start: The Nag's Head, Main Road, Pontesbury, SY5 0QD.

Parking: At the Nag's Head with the permission of the proprietor, or at the car park for Earl's Hill and start at Point 3 Sat Nav SY5 0UH.

Map: OS Explorer 241 Shrewsbury and 216 Welshpool.
Grid Ref: SJ406060.

Terrain: Field and woodland paths, quiet lanes.

Near the pretty village of Pontesbury the infant Pontesford Brook makes a dramatic passage through a wooded gorge, even hurling itself over a couple of metres of waterfall, before reaching calmer pastures to the north. Here the Rea Brook wanders more sedately between alder and willow before forces are combined to head for Shrewsbury and the Severn. Following both brooks through their varied terrain, there are no stiles to negotiate on this well-signed walk, so why not take your four-legged friend along too?

Pontesbury 9

THE NAG'S HEAD is a recently modernised hostelry with a relaxed feel. In the centre, flames leap cheerfully from a gas fire in a glass case, attractively dividing restaurant area from bar, where dogs are welcomed. Wooden panelling complements wooden floors. In summer, the garden's plentiful seating invites you to unwind over a pint of Shropshire ale and the wide-ranging menu as you enjoy the prospect of Earl's Hill.
🌐 nagsheadpontesbury.co.uk ☎ 01743 790060.

The Walk

1 Leaving the **Nag's Head**, turn right along the main road and in a few metres cross over to continue down **Bogey Lane**.

2 Approaching the school, take the lane on the left, and at the top of the rise, go through a gate on the left to cross a small field. Through another gate, turn left on a rough track to meet the road. Bearing right now, and climbing, you soon reach the car park for **Earl's Hill** on the left.

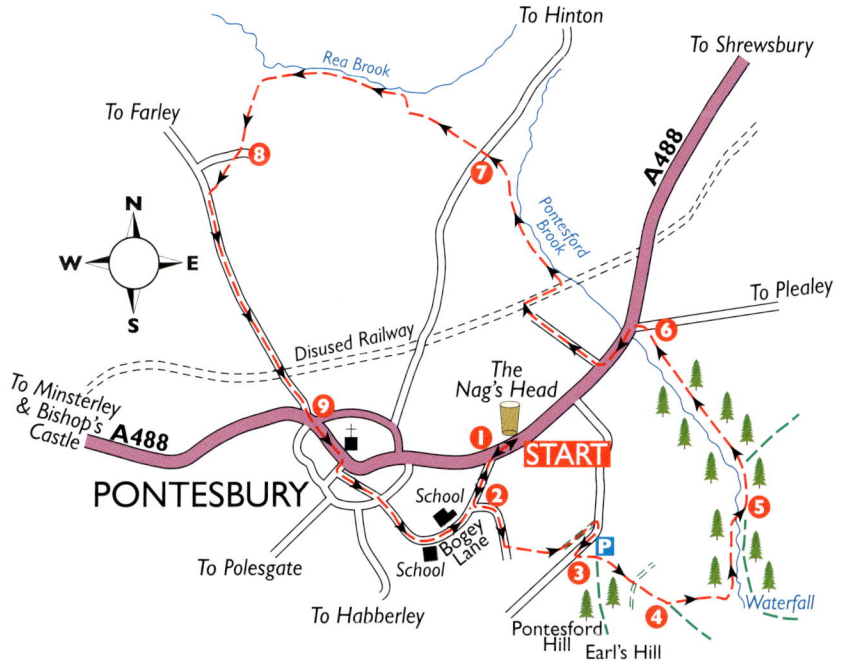

45

Shropshire Pub Walks

3 Walk through the car parking area and where the broad path curves right, keep left, immediately dropping down to a kissing gate into a field. Cross the field to a lane, then go right and almost immediately left to enter a field with a large pond on the left. Bear right up the slope to another field gate.

4 Head diagonally left across this huge field, going past a big oak tree to a wooden kissing gate beside a pond on the edge of the wood. On its far side, steep steps lead down to the **Pontesford Brook**, with the **Lyd Holes waterfall** just to the right. When you have taken in the scene, turn back and continue alongside the brook to go through a wooden gate into a field. Keeping beside the brook, a gate on the right allows you to cross a wooden bridge to climb the slope on the far side.

5 At the path junction at the top of the climb, go left on a path along the woodland edge. Ignore the first stile on your right, but keep to this path as it leaves and re-enters the wood before finally escaping into a field and continuing along its edge to a lane. Turn left here and walk down to the main road.

6 Go left on the road and in some 200 metres, cross over to continue up Back Lane. In around ¼ mile you reach a broad cross-track, which in fact is the route of a disused railway. Go right on this, and in around 250 metres, go down steps to join a path running alongside **Pontesford Brook** again.

7 This pleasant path curves round to end at a lane, where diagonally left, another field path soon leads across a wooden footbridge to the banks of the **Rea Brook**. Follow it to the left before finally turning away on a well-marked path that dodges in and out of fields on sleeper bridges over ditches and eventually reaches a lane.

8 Across the lane bear right to a gate in the field hedge and

Pontesbury

maintain the direction to arrive at a road. Turn left and walk down to **Pontesbury**.

9 Cross the main road directly and continue as the road curves left until the church is on your left. Turn right here, and take the first left (**Stallion Lane**). At its top bear left and immediately right walking uphill to continue between two schools. Reaching the edge of the playing fields you are at Point 2 and can retrace your steps ahead down the lane to the pub, or turn right and follow the Point 2 directions to the **Earl's Hill car park**.

Place of Interest Nearby

Earl's Hill Nature Reserve (see Point 3) has recently been extended to include adjacent Pontesford Hill. Both hills are volcanic in origin, and their sharp profile is said to resemble that of a sleeping dragon. The view from the open summit of Earl's Hill is stunning, but down in the valley below there are primroses and bluebells in springtime, and a wide variety of birds enjoying the native woodland on the banks of the stream. Entry is free.

Walk 10
COUND

Distance: 3½ miles (5.5 km)

Start: The Riverside Inn, Cound, SY5 6AF.

Parking: At the Riverside Inn for patrons. Alternatively, start at Point 5 in the village of Cound, where there is parking at the Guildhall. Sat Nav SY5 6EW – donation requested.

Map: OS Explorer 241 Shrewsbury. **Grid Ref:** SJ570050.

Terrain: Good field and woodland paths. Several stiles.

There are a couple of lovely field paths on this walk, the sort that are clear-cut and firm underfoot, weaving their way through banks of rippling corn (in season) while leading your eye to tantalising distant horizons. They are not the highlight, though, by any means. That accolade must go to the gentle remote valley of the Coundmoor Brook. If you should take this walk early in the year you will find the valley filled with snowdrops, making it

Cound

even more delightful. You might also want to take a pause in the little hamlet of Cound where the beautiful 13th-century church houses a Norman font and medieval wall painting.

THE PUB — **THE RIVERSIDE INN** is a popular Chef & Brewer pub just off the A458. Driving past you would have no idea that the River Severn was so close, but there it is, right outside the windows of the pub. In fact the river makes a big bend here, the only point at which it touches the road, and the lovely gardens and patios of the Riverside make the most of it. On a fine summer's day there could be nowhere more pleasant to enjoy your pint. But the Riverside caters for winter, too, with no fewer than five open fires in its bar and dining rooms. And almost everywhere there is a view of that river. 'Wagging tails are welcome' at the Riverside, and in the attractive wood-panelled bar dogs are offered a biscuit while their owners deliberate over the varied and changing menu. ⊕ chefandbrewer.com/pubs/shropshire/riverside-inn/ ☎ 01743 296613.

Shropshire Pub Walks

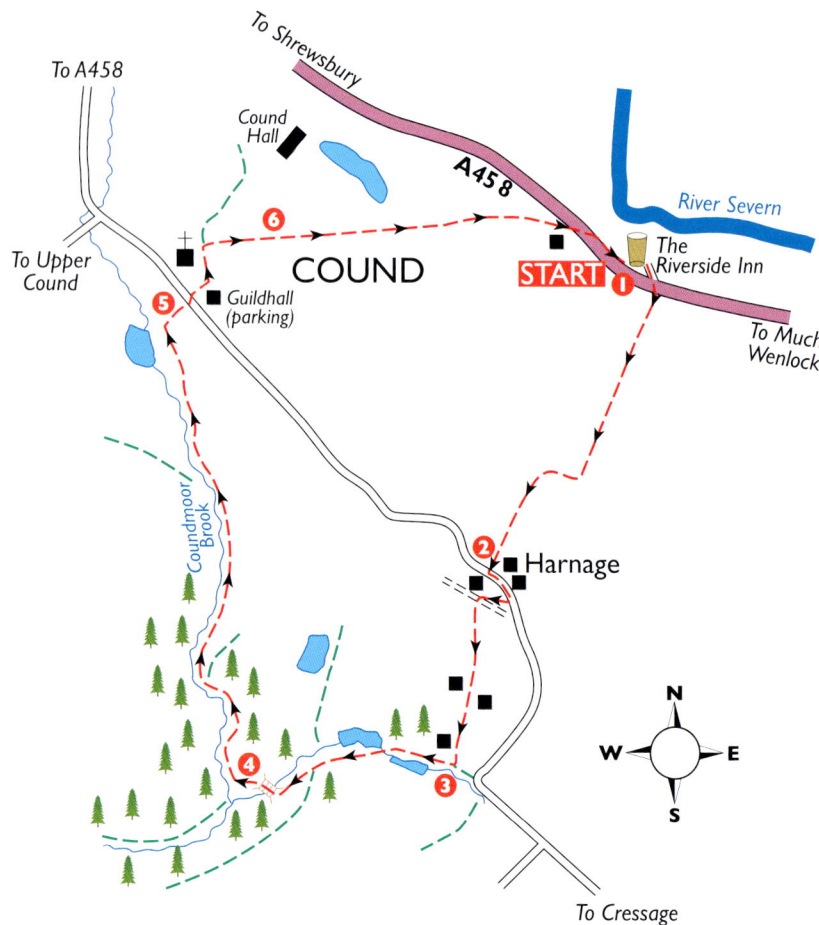

The Walk

1 Leave the **Riverside Inn** through its car park and walk up the access road to the **A458**. Cross this road to a footpath sign just to the left on the far side. The path now takes you up beside a house and then on across the open field, maintaining its direction to a stile in the hedge on the far side. Once over the stile, turn right along the field edge, then bear left on a farm track leading out to a lane in the village of **Harnage**.

Cound 10

2 Go left on the lane, and just beyond the last house, look for a byway sign pointing into the small field on your right. Going diagonally right across this field you reach a barn, and beyond it, a hard-surfaced track. Across the track a clear field path runs down towards houses. Pass between them on the signed path, crossing an entrance drive and continuing over a stile and through a gate, finally descending into a field beside a house.

3 At the bottom of the slope do not cross the stream but turn right on a wide track, keeping a large pond on your left. At its end bear left to have the next pond on your right, and continue through the field just below the woodland edge, well above the water. At the very far end of the field, the now indistinct path descends to cross the stream on a wooden footbridge. Turn left on the far side and continue to a track T-junction in the valley.

4 Turn right on the obvious wide track and where it eventually bends away right, keep ahead through a gate into a field. Now simply carry on following the **Coundmoor Brook** through successive fields until a fence ahead means you can go no more. Turn right here and walk up the field to a signed stile beside a high beech hedge. The path now quickly leads to the road in the village of **Cound**.

5 Cross the road to walk down between the low brick Guildhall and a second-hand bookshop and bear left at the end to arrive at the bottom of the churchyard. Here a path on the right leads to two wooden kissing gates. Go through the right-hand one and bear left across the corner of the field to another kissing gate beside a chestnut tree. The fence between two fields stands ahead. Enter the left-hand field and walk down with the fence on your right to cross a stile in the hedge opposite.

6 A lovely long field path now stretches ahead, passing **Cound Hall** on your left and eventually reaching a small metal gate before a house. Through this, continue on the well-marked path to emerge beside the **A458**. Cross over and turn right along the verge to the **Riverside Inn**.

Shropshire Pub Walks

Place of Interest Nearby

Four miles way to the south-west, down the most winding of country lanes, and well-concealed in the greenery, is **Acton Burnell Castle**. Dating from the late 13th century, it is no more than a shell today, and all the more evocative for that. The castle was built by Bishop Burnell, Edward I's Lord Chancellor, and two Parliaments were held in the castle's tithe barn in 1283 and 1285. The early Parliament has the distinction of being the first ever in which commoners were represented. Although cared for by English Heritage, Acton Burnell sees few visitors so you may well find yourself standing alone in the handsome red sandstone ruins as you imagine the scene. The castle is open daily until dusk, with free entry. Sat Nav SY5 7PE.
⊕ english-heritage.org.uk/visit/places/acton-burnell-castle/history

Walk 11
KEMBERTON

Distance: 4 miles (6.4 km)

Start: The Masons Arms, Hall Lane, Kemberton, TF11 9LQ.

Parking: At the Masons Arms for patrons, otherwise on quiet roadsides in the village.

Map: OS Explorer 242 Telford. **Grid Ref:** SJ727044.

Terrain: Field and woodland paths. One short gradual ascent. Several stiles.

Kemberton is one of those villages where you are as likely to encounter a horse as a car, and contented cats take their midday siestas in the middle of the road. And yet, the bustling industry of Telford is no more than a stone's throw away.

The peaceful scene continues into the countryside around where just a few fields away the Wesley Brook wanders lazily through woodland on its way to join the River Worfe. The path through those woods is lovely at any time of year, but in springtime the display of bluebells, stitchwort, red campion, and more is just stunning. The walk here takes in the best of the woodland scene, but it also passes an impressive old watermill, and then climbs a not-too-lofty hill for a fine view

Shropshire Pub Walks

of distant summits. It's a delightful cameo amble that is just perfect for Sunday morning before a robust lunch at the Masons Arms.

THE PUB

THE MASONS ARMS feels fresh and airy, with modern and comfortable upholstered seating and light wood furniture. The large bar area, where dogs are welcomed, has an attractive open fire with copper cowling, while there's yet another fire in the more formal dining area set to one side. In summer the garden comes into its own, with a painted shelter and tastefully coloured brollies on tables overlooking the fields. Tapas are popular at the Masons, as indeed is Sunday lunch, and there's a wide menu with a good range of cask ales on tap.

🌐 masonsarmskemberton.co.uk ☎ 01952 684019.

The Walk

❶ Leaving the inn car park, turn right and walk down to the T-junction in the village. Ahead of you there is a footpath sign pointing through a gate on to a grassy track between houses. A few metres down that track, go through a kissing gate on the left and continue downhill beside the fence, turning left at the bottom of the field to go through another gate. Arriving at a track, turn left to meet a lane. Again turn left and continue some 50 metres to a fingerpost and stile on the right.

❷ Head directly across the field, aiming for a lone oak tree on the far side. Cross a farm track and keep ahead to pass the tree and carry on downhill, where the path bends right. A stile now gives access to a track which leads to a gravelled lane. Turn left on the lane and follow it to some houses on the site of the old **Kemberton Mill**.

❸ Go through a kissing gate on the left here to cross the brook

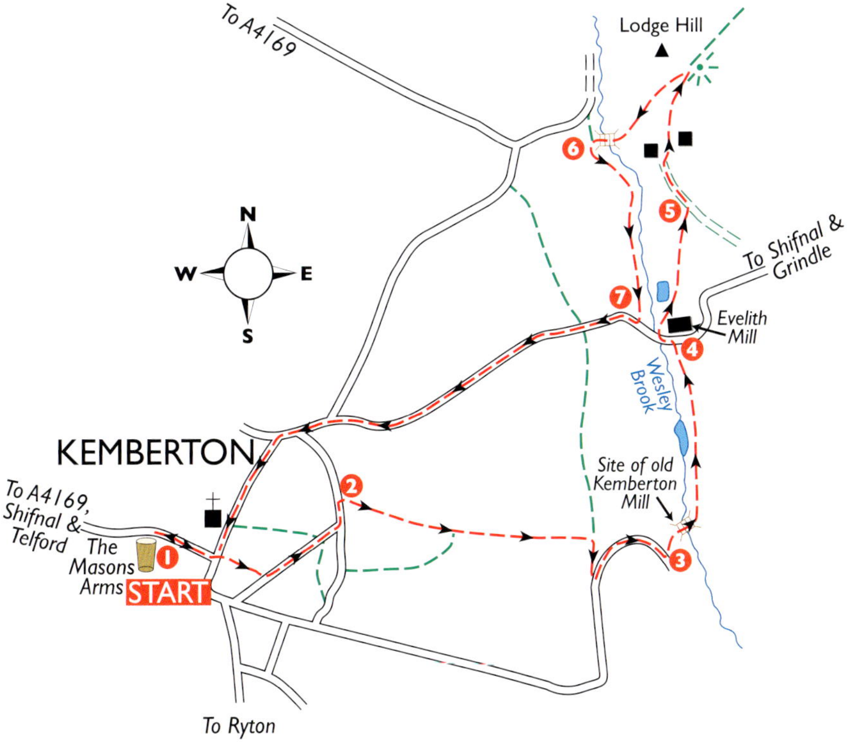

Kemberton 11

on two footbridges and bear left on the path into the woods. This lovely path now parallels the stream, and in springtime is garlanded with wild flowers. At one point wide ponds can be glimpsed through the trees. Eventually the path reaches a road at **Evelith Mill**, a watermill dating from the mid-19th century.

4 Go left on the road and very soon, go right into the grounds of the mill. Signs direct you between buildings to climb again on the far side of the brook,

55

Shropshire Pub Walks

from where you can admire a fine pond. Continue on the path, which finally leaves the wood and after a couple of stiles, meets a gravelled track.

5 Turn left, passing the houses, then in front of the farm, bear right, as signed, to pass between buildings. A stile here leads to a faint grassy path climbing **Lodge Hill** (114m) ahead. Where the path meets a fence, turn sharp left to descend – but just take a few minutes to survey the distant scene first.

To the south-west, just left of the fence line, all Shropshire's highest hills stand in line. To the north, the edge of Shifnal and its church can be seen across the fields.

Following the fence downhill, you arrive at a kissing gate into the woods again. After a steep descent, the path crosses the brook on a footbridge.

6 Once over the footbridge, turn sharp left. The path soon enters woodland again, and then continues along its edge, high above the brook. After some 500 metres, this pleasant path reaches a road.

7 Turn right on the road. Keep ahead, ignoring all side turnings, for almost a mile to pass **Kemberton church**. The next turn on the right will then return you to the **Masons Arms**.

Place of Interest Nearby

Some ten minutes' drive south from Kemberton will have you on the **River Severn at Coalport**. The story of the village's famous chinaware is told in a museum on the site, with some magnificent exhibits, and a little hands-on as well. You could enjoy a cup of coffee at the adjacent **Youth Hostel's excellent café**, and take a stroll beside the pretty canal, along which those fine china items were once transported. And within walking distance are more interesting sites, the **Tar Tunnel** and **Jackfield Tile Museum** – after which it's only a short drive into historic **Ironbridge** itself. Sat Nav TF8 7HT.

🌐 ironbridge.org.uk/explore/coalport-china-museum

Walk 12
QUATFORD

Distance: 5 miles (8 km)

Start: The Danery, Kidderminster Road, Quatford, WV15 6QJ.

Parking: The Danery is set in a big lay-by with access from the A442. There is ample parking in the lay-by.

Map: OS Explorer 218 Wyre Forest & Kidderminster.
Grid Ref: SO738905.

Terrain: Easy woodland paths, quiet lanes. No stiles. Dog-friendly.

The walk here visits Comer Woods, a fairly extensive forest that is part of the Dudmaston Estate. Dudmaston is in the hands of the National Trust, and in Comer they have marked out a network of varied paths, from wide gravelly trails suitable for young cyclists to tiny footpaths winding off into wilder parts for those who want to get off-the-beaten-track a bit more. Every path

Shropshire Pub Walks

looks enticing, but the route here keeps to the more main paths on which you won't get disorientated (something it's very easy to do in Comer Woods!) and takes you down to three lakes in a valley at the lower end of the wood. Comer Woods has something for every season – wild flowers and rhododendrons in spring, butterflies in summer, rich colours and fungi in autumn – and it's just a short stride from the village of Quatford.

THE PUB — **THE DANERY** is easy to miss, even though it's on a main road. Sitting in a lay-by well below traffic level, there's no eye-catching sign to lure you aside. But for all its obscure location, the Danery is an attractive inn, festooned in wisteria in springtime and well-decked with baskets of bright summery blooms. Eating outside amid all this is a real pleasure, and the shrub-filled beer garden with children's play area is also deservedly popular. Inside, the building is clearly old, with low ceilings, tiny rooms, and alcoves. The menu is not exotic, but food is of a high quality, and service is friendly. And is it

Quatford 12

dog-friendly? Well, for six days of the week it is, but on Sunday all four-legged friends must remain outside 'for health and safety reasons'!
🌐 facebook.com/thedanerybridgnorth ☎ 01746 762255.

The Walk

1 From the **Danery**, walk up to the other end of the lay-by where steps lead up to the church. Do not go up them but turn right on the track which climbs between sandstone banks. After the last house, a path climbs the bank on the left to a kissing gate. In the field beyond, turn right alongside the hedge, then cut across diagonally to a gate at the top left-hand corner beside the wood. Turn right along the edge of the field, then continue on a wide track inside the edge of the wood.

2 Meeting a road, turn right, and walk downhill for some 600 metres. Here a gap beside a metal gate gives access to **Comer Wood**. Take the most left of three wide paths and simply keep to it, ignoring inviting turnings on either side. After almost ½ mile you pass an old cottage buried deep in the woods, and not long afterwards, arrive at a five-way junction.

3 Ignore the sharp left turn here and take the next on the left, indicated on a wooden signpost as the **'Explorer Trail'**. This broad path now soon descends into a valley. At the junction at the bottom of the hill, go right and walk through the valley to a junction beside a seat.

4 Bear left here and quite soon you will have glimpses of water between the trees on the right. Three lakes lie in the valley, little paths run down to the water's edge, and there are seats from where you can admire the scene. Keep ahead on the main path, ignoring all others, and eventually the last lake is passed. Some 300 metres farther on, you arrive at a barrier at the edge of the woods.

5 Turn sharp left on an earthen track, initially between high banks. After ½ mile you come to a farm and pass between its buildings to reach a tarmacked lane. Keep ahead on this for 500 metres to arrive at a path crossing.

Shropshire Pub Walks

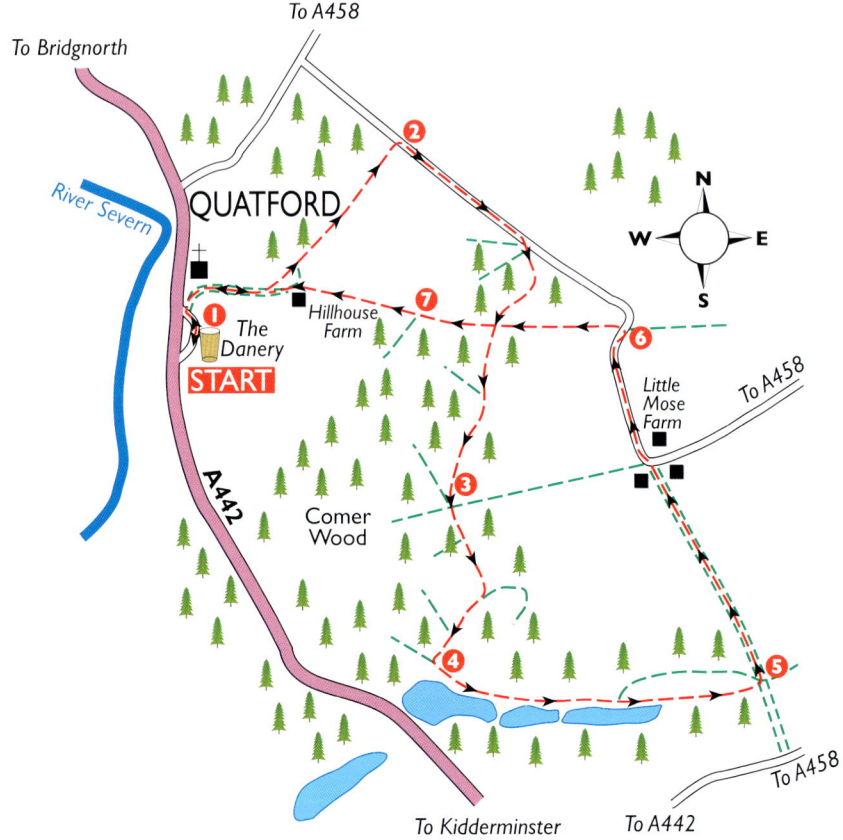

6 Turn left on a cross-field path heading for the woods. At the woodland edge, a much narrower path dives through the trees to arrive at a junction with the wide track you took in Point 2. Cross straight over that wide track on a lesser path that now descends into a valley, crosses yet another wide track and climbs.

7 Where your path now bears left at the top of the hill, leave it and go maybe 50 metres farther on to find a metal gate into a field on the right. Cross the field directly, to where another gate takes you alongside a farm. Having passed the buildings, a kissing gate on the left admits you to the drive in front of the house. Keep straight ahead down the access road and very soon you will find

Quatford 12

yourself descending to the church at **Quatford** again, with **The Danery** nearby.

Place of Interest Nearby

Comer Woods belongs to the National Trust managed **Dudmaston estate**, and just down the road is the house itself. Dudmaston offers two particular treats – outside are colourful gardens, woodland walks, and a huge lake, while inside are the art galleries. The latter are attributable to Sir George and Lady Labouchere who lived here in the last century; she was a botanical artist, he collected modern art for its own sake. Well-known names like Hepworth, Rodin and Matisse stand alongside others you may not have heard of. And, of course, there are more treats in the National Trust café! Sat Nav WV15 6QN.
⊕ nationaltrust.org.uk/dudmaston

Walk 13
MUCH WENLOCK

Distance: 4½ miles (7.4 km)

Start: The Talbot Inn, High Street, Much Wenlock, TF13 6AA.

Parking: The Talbot Inn has no parking. The most convenient (paying) car park is off St Mary's Road on the south side of town – follow signs. From there a quick walk through the George Shut has you in the High Street with the Talbot to your left. Alternatively, you can start the walk at the free car park at Point 2. Sat Nav TF13 6DH.

Map: OS Explorers 242 Telford and 217 The Long Mynd.
Grid Ref: SO622998.

Terrain: Field and woodland paths with around 80 metres on a busy main road. No stiles, dog-friendly.

'On Wenlock Edge the wood's in trouble', so begins one of the best-known poems in Housman's *A Shropshire Lad*, in which he is depicting autumn, but evocative Wenlock Edge has inspired many references in literature, song, and art. The Edge is a steep,

Much Wenlock 13

thickly-wooded limestone escarpment that was once a coral reef under a tropical sea, and would seem to be as well known for its geological as for its artistic connections. The walk here takes in a long section of that Edge and, in winter at least, you can peer through the trees to pick out the farms and hamlets way below.

Much Wenlock itself is a fascinating town, a place of antique shops, tearooms, and galleries – and has another claim to fame in that a 19th-century doctor in the town was the instigator and inspiration for the modern series of the Olympic Games. Don't miss visiting the little museum in town for the full story.

THE PUB **THE TALBOT INN** originated somewhere back in the 14th century as a building known as Abbot's Hall. By the 17th century it was certainly a hostelry and James I is known to have spent a night there. Today the Talbot has an unassuming presence on the High Street but once inside you can really appreciate its warmth and antiquity with low ceilings and open fires.  Best of all is the courtyard, wooden seating sheltered between black and white half-timbered walls, well-decked with floral displays in summertime. Your canine companion will be allowed no farther than this lovely courtyard, but given fair weather, it will hardly be a hardship!
⊕ thetalbotinnmuchwenlock.co.uk ☎ 01952 727077.

The Walk

❶ Leaving the **Talbot Inn**, turn left and walk away from town to the main road junction. Keep straight ahead here, on the pavement beside the **A458 Shrewsbury Road**. Ignore the first left turn (**SP Craven Arms**) and continue 400 metres to the second (**SP Church Stretton**). Some 100 metres up this road, take a small road on the right signed to **Blakeway Hollow**. The road becomes a rough track, and just beyond a gateway, there is a car park on the left.

❷ Continue up long stony **Blakeway Hollow** to a wooden gate on

Shropshire Pub Walks

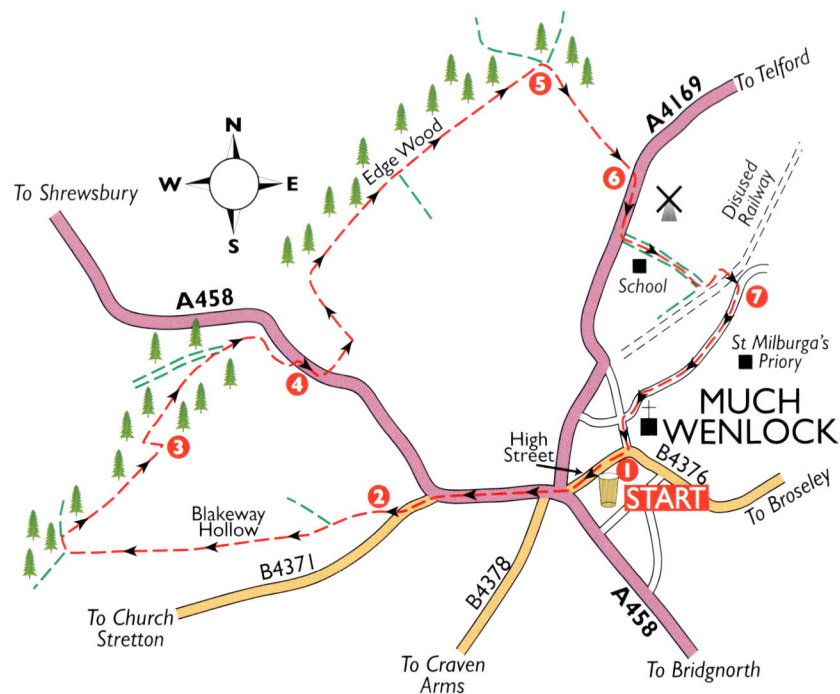

the left at the top of the slope admitting you to a field. Across this another gate gives access to the wood. Turn right to pass through another gate, and at the track junction, go diagonally right on a bridleway. After a few metres, a much lesser signed path leaves on the right to continue between field and wood. Stick with this until, in a field with undulations, you find a gate in the angle of the wood.

❸ A sign welcomes you to **Blakeway Coppice**. Go right on a path dipping and climbing, eventually reaching a T-junction with a broad track. Turn right and descend to the **A458**.

❹ Turn right and take great care – you have something like 80 metres on this narrow busy road before crossing to a kissing gate on the left. Through this gate, continue through the wood, turning left in front of a gate on a path that climbs along the woodland edge. At the top, turn right to walk along **Wenlock Edge** with

Much Wenlock 13

the wood falling steeply on your left and, in winter at least, glimpses of farms and settlements way below.

5 After almost a mile, with the path now dropping steeply, you arrive at a track junction at the woodland edge. Turn sharply right away from the wood on a path with the hedge on your right. This continues between a hedge and fence, and, through a kissing gate, descends across a field to meet the **A4169**.

6 Cross the road and turn right for about 100 metres to find an entrance into **Windmill Hill** field on the left. The pleasant track passes a school and then parkland to a junction at its corner. Go left here and negotiate steps to cross a disused railway line. Beyond it, the path meets a lane.

7 Go right and continue ½ mile into town, passing **St Milburga's Priory**. At the road junction, go left, passing the church on your left and the birthplace of Dr William Penny Brookes on your right. Take the next right for the clock tower, **High Street** and the **Talbot** inn.

Place of Interest Nearby

St Milburga's Priory is passed at the end of this walk, and is worth returning to for a visit. Around the end of the 7th century, King Merewahl of Mercia built a monastery here, and it was his daughter Milburga that became its second abbess, and was subsequently canonised. Some four centuries later, the Cluniacs had taken over the monastery, and in rebuilding the church, were fortunate enough to unearth the relics of St Milburga. The monastery became a place of pilgrimage, and fame and wealth followed. Today you can view the remains of those ornate Cluniac buildings in a truly beautiful setting.
⊕ english-heritage.org.uk/visit/places/wenlock-priory

Walk 14
Picklescott

Distance: 4 miles (6.4 km)

Start: The Bottle and Glass, Picklescott, SY6 6NR.

Parking: At the pub with the permission of the proprietor. Otherwise there is ample parking at the village hall, about 200 metres up the hill on the road to Smethcott (donation requested).

Map: OS Explorer 217 The Long Mynd & Wenlock Edge.
Grid Ref: SO435994.

Terrain: Field and woodland paths. Quiet lanes. Some paths can be boggy after heavy rain, particularly the bridleway in Point 2 and sections in the valleys. Several stiles so only suitable for dogs that can be lifted over them.

You'll need a good pair of boots for this walk, because water running off the hills can create some boggy terrain. But if you have those boots, this walk is a classic, showcasing in just a few miles the farmland, deep bluebell-filled valleys, intimate villages and centuries-old churches of this part of Shropshire. Picklescott

Picklescott 14

is situated where the land first begins to rise at the northern edge of the Long Mynd, and the narrow twisting lanes that lead to it emphasise its remoteness. Once here though, you can't fail to be captivated by that lovely old pub at the heart of an off-the-beaten-track corner of Shropshire.

THE PUB — **THE BOTTLE AND GLASS** is a gem not to be missed. Genuinely old and yet very well cared for, it gives you the feeling of being instantly transported back in time. The bar with its sagging beams, flagstone floor, high settles and open fire, were it not for its discreet electric lighting, would surely take you back to pre-industrial times. And the two tiny wood-panelled dining rooms with heavy oak furniture do nothing to break the spell. Dogs will feel very much at home in this cosy rustic setting. The Bottle and Glass may have kept its 17th-century charm, but you are jetted right back to the present day with the menu, which largely features local produce and is enticingly wide-ranging to say the least.
🌐 www.bottleandglasspicklescott.co.uk ☎ 01694 751252.

Shropshire Pub Walks

The Walk

1 From the **Bottle and Glass**, walk down to the road junction in the centre of the village and continue on the road signed to **Betchcott**. After around ½ mile, having passed a farm on the left, look out for a signed bridleway on the same side.

2 The grassy ride soon passes through a gate in front of **Batchcott Hall Farm** and immediately bends right to descend through woodland. Some 200 metres after emerging from the trees, find a metal gate on the right bearing an inconspicuous footpath sign.

3 Go through the gate and continue along the right-hand edge of a long field to reach a stile. The path now winds down a long slope to plunge into the woodland of **Betchcott Hollow**. Cross the brook on a wooden footbridge before following the path as it climbs steeply up the opposite bank.

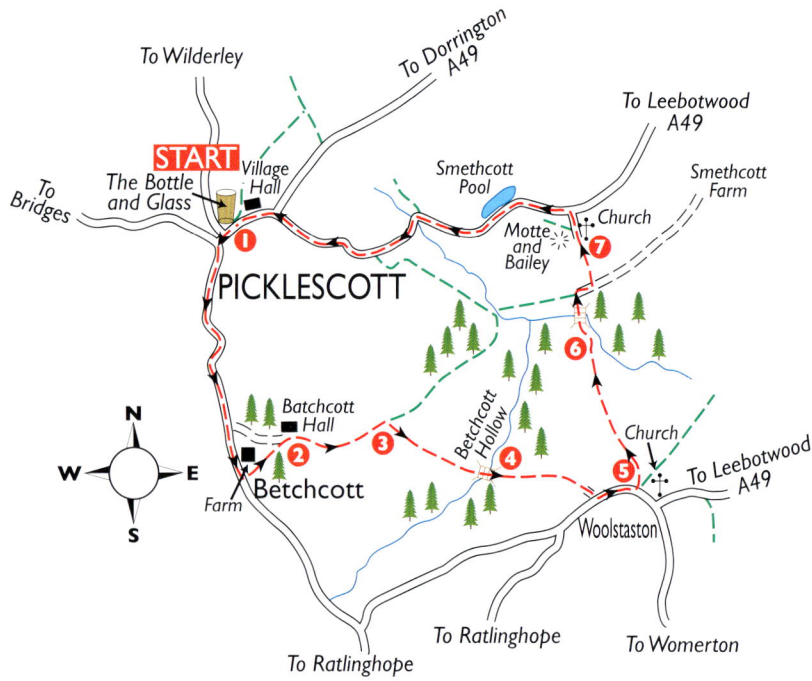

Picklescott 14

St Michael and All Angels, Woolstaston

4 Cross over two stiles now, then aim for the far left-hand corner of the field beyond. Here a metal gate takes you onto a track beside a field that soon emerges on a rough lane. Continue to meet a tarmacked road and turn left to enter the village of **Woolstaston**.

5 As the road descends, a wooden signpost points you up steps on the left to arrive on the wide lawns of a handsome house. Here a gate on the right will admit you to **Woolstaston Church**.

St Michael and All Angels at Woolstaston retains features dating back to the 12th century, with Romanesque carving on the south doorway. The bell tower was rebuilt and the church re-roofed with handmade Shropshire slate some 30 years ago.

Back on the lawn, climb to a stile at its highest point on the left-hand side. The path now hugs the left-hand edge of the next short field, followed by two more fields. At a gateway here, an arrow points diagonally right to a stile just visible beside woodland across the next field.

6 Beyond the stile, the path weaves its way down the wooded slope, finally crossing **Betchcott Brook** once more on a wooden bridge. A short climb now takes you over a stile to a path junction. Go right here, finally emerging through a gate onto a wide track. Turn right again, and in 30 metres or so, go left on a bridleway ascending between hedges to arrive at **Smethcott Church**.

St Michael's at Smethcott is Norman in origin, although it was largely refurbished in the 1850s. The field opposite the church contains the remains of a motte and bailey fortification with a commanding view over the surrounding countryside. A stile in the hedge further down the road allows you access.

7 The Ordnance Survey map shows a path through this motte and bailey field, but sadly it is no longer passable. Instead, walk from the church to the road at the bottom of the hill and turn left. After passing **Smethcott Pool**, another path on the right would appear to be a shorter route back to **Picklescott**, but again it is blocked by vegetation. Simply keep ahead on the little-used road, bearing left at the junction, to pass the **Village Hall** and descend to the **Bottle and Glass**.

Place of Interest Nearby

Heading from Picklescott towards Shrewsbury, just beyond the village of Dorrington you will pass a turning to **Lyth Hill Country Park**, a site of open grassland and oak woodland. Not that high in itself, Lyth Hill is nevertheless a splendid viewpoint, and a toposcope allows you to identify all the south-Shropshire ranges. Mary Webb, author of 1924 novel *Precious Bane*, lived on Lyth Hill for the last ten years of her life and it is said to have inspired her later works. Sat Nav SY3 0BT.

Walk 15
STIPERSTONES

Distance: 4 miles (6.6 km)

Start: The Stiperstones Inn, Stiperstones, SY5 0LZ.

Parking: At the Stiperstones Inn with the permission of the proprietor. Otherwise, park roadside in the village or drive on almost a mile to a wide gravelled parking area on a left-hand bend and start the walk at Point 2.

Map: OS Explorer 216 Welshpool and Montgomery.
Grid Ref: SJ363004.

Terrain: Field paths, gravelled tracks. Gradual climb to summit and steep descent. Several stiles.

Stiperstones is a colourful place. In spring this walk is a symphony in yellow; daffodils lining the banks the length of Stipersones village are followed by hillsides blazing bright with gorse. Later in the year those same heights are carpeted in purple heather.

Shropshire Pub Walks

The views are as memorable as the colours on this walk. Yes, you will have to work for them, be in no doubt, but the long sweep of the plains to the north, with conical Corndon and adjacent Stapeley Hill to the west, and the shadowy far-distant mountains beyond make it well worth the effort. There are nearer views as well – the long ridge of Stiperstones bristling with outcrops of quartz, Stiperstones village nestling in the valley below you, and disused Tankerville lead mine tucked in a fold in the hills. And with all that, you mustn't forget to listen out for the clankings of Wild Edric, a Saxon chief, imprisoned with his men in the disused mines below your feet, waiting to come out in England's hour of need. Stiperstones is above all a land of legend!

THE STIPERSTONES INN is every walker's idea of heaven, an old low-beamed pub serving real ales and hearty, affordable meals throughout the day. There could not be a book of pub walks in Shropshire without including it. In winter there are open fires and log burners to dry clothes and thaw out frozen fingers; in summer,

cheerfully painted tables in the beer garden complement the sunshine. Dogs are, of course, welcome in the bar – and for those who would like a little more formality with their dining, there are separate small rooms that provide just that. Locally sourced food is the order of the day at the Stiperstones, and their whinberry pie is legendary. Every year, hundreds of pounds of berries are picked from the hills behind to make sure it is always on the menu, so don't miss it!
🌐 stiperstonesinn.co.uk ☎ 01743 791327.

The Walk

1 With your back to the pub, turn left and walk through

Stiperstones 15

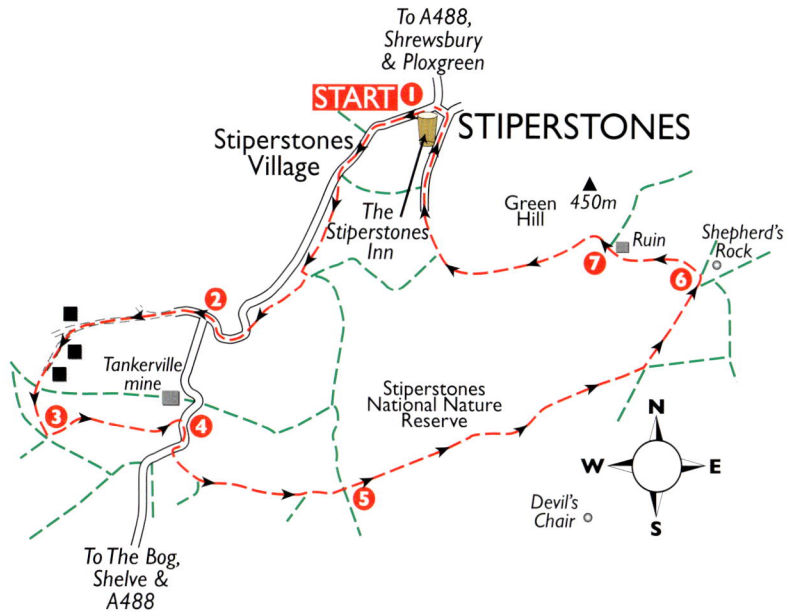

Stiperstones village on the road. Just after the last house on the left, a signed path climbs the bank beside you to reach a stile into a field. Turn right and climb steeply beside the hedge until a waymarked post is reached. Arrows point left here to direct you over a stile into the **Reserve**. A few metres to the right now, a bridleway gate leads onto a path descending to the road. Go left and walk up to the next bend with its parking area.

❷ On the bend, take the wide gravelled track dipping down on the right to pass a coach depot. With the track climbing again, keep left at the fork to soon find yourself in a sort of coal yard. At the top right corner of this, signs direct you over a stile onto the hillside behind. Go right for a few metres, then at a marked post, left up a very steep bank to join a wide gravelled track. Turn left and continue climbing to reach a stile at the top of the hill. It's worth looking back at the view from here.

❸ Turn left alongside the hedge and walk down the field with the **Devil's Chair** rocks on Stiperstones directly ahead and Manstone

Shropshire Pub Walks

and **Cranberry Rocks** stretching out to the right. At the bottom left corner of the field, cross a stile onto a narrow track descending under a big holly bush and continue with views of **Tankerville mine** on the left. At the track fork, head left downhill on a path that soon rises to the road.

4 Go right on the road, and just around the bend, take a broad track signed as a footpath and no through road. Reaching a house that was once a chapel, turn left and continue climbing, keeping on the main path (left at all junctions) to reach a gate leading onto the **Stiperstones Reserve**.

5 Continue ahead, gently uphill, and in about ¾ mile you will arrive at a cairn on the summit path of Stiperstones. Turn left here on a stony path that passes right of a rocky outcrop to reach a cairn and major path junction in front of conical **Shepherd's Rock**.

6 Turn left now on a grassy track that soon begins to descend quite steeply. Keep with the path and at length arrive at a track junction in a grassy meadow in front of a small ruined building.

7 Keep left, and continue descending the valley until eventually you leave the **Reserve**. The track continues for maybe half a mile, passing houses and becoming tarmacked before reaching a T-junction. Just to the left here is the **Stiperstones Inn**.

Place of Interest Nearby

A few miles away to the west, and visible on this walk, is flat-topped **Stapeley Hill**, at whose foot is a Bronze Age stone circle known as **Mitchell's Fold**. Only 30 stones remain of an original 60, the largest of which is thought to have marked the entrance. The hill beyond has ring cairns and more prehistoric remains – and of course there's a legend attached, but you'll have to go there to read all about it. Sat Nav SY15 6DE. ⊕ english-heritage.org.uk/visit/places/mitchells-fold-stone-circle.

Walk 16
All Stretton

Distance: 4½ miles (7.2 km)

Start: The Yew Tree, Shrewsbury Road, All Stretton, SY6 6HG.

Parking: At the Yew Tree for patrons with the permission of the proprietor. Otherwise, turn up the road signed to the Village Hall (about 50 metres from the Yew Tree) and continue into Batch Valley where there is National Trust parking (donation suggested). Sat Nav SY6 6JW.

Map: OS Explorer 217 The Long Mynd. **Grid Ref:** SO459954.

Terrain: Grassy and stony paths, quiet road. Steepish climb near the beginning and 'sting in the tail' climb and descent at the end. No stiles. Sheep grazing almost throughout.

Here you are on the Long Mynd, where the geological features have curious names, and the deep valleys characteristic of the eastern side of the ridge are referred to as 'batches' or 'hollows'.

Shropshire Pub Walks

This walk actually begins in a place known as Batch Valley, which would therefore seem to be a classic case of tautology!

Beyond Batch Valley there are certainly a lot of ups-and-downs on this ramble, but they bring their reward – splendid distant views from the summit of Plush Hill, the thick vegetation of the particularly deep valley called Gogbatch and the open common or heathland where you may be lucky enough to see ponies grazing. These ponies, and the sheep too, belong to local farmers known as Commoners, and each flock will instinctively keep to its own terrain, called a heft, although there are no fences to divide them. The territorial information is simply passed from ewe to lamb down the generations.

THE PUB

THE YEW TREE reflects its 17th-century vintage with black beams and rugged supporting timbers. The traditional bar, where dogs are welcomed, benefits from a log burner, while in the dining area, a large inglenook fireplace lends atmosphere. The whole has a cosy feel, but the Yew Tree really comes into its own in the summer with lots of outdoor seating on both patio and grass as well as a large oak pavilion offering shelter and yet another bar. It's the perfect setting for enjoying a homemade pizza baked in their own wood-fired oven.

🌐 yewtree-allstretton.co.uk ☎ 01694 328593.

All Stretton 16

The Walk

❶ Leaving the **Yew Tree car park**, turn right and in about 50 metres, and go right signed to **'Village Hall'**. After about 400 metres you reach a cattle grid beyond which there are two small parking lots and a sign welcoming you to **Batch Valley**. Continue up the valley, cross the stream, and keep ahead on the main track to cross it once more. Stick with the main path, which becomes narrower, to pass a house and reach a junction of valleys.

❷ Here a post marked **'Jinlye'** points you back up the hillside on the right. Climb the narrow track with its splendid views to emerge at another junction on the summit, in front of the garden gate of **Plush Hill**. Going right here, you will quickly meet a tarmacked road. Turn left and continue until you are almost opposite the front gate of Plush Hill, where there is a magnificent view across the Shropshire Plain, with the Wrekin and the Lawley rising far away to the right.

❸ Look out across the common land to see a wide path climbing the gentle rise diagonally right. Branch right off the road here and descend to join that track. Keeping straight ahead now you will reach a stream and vegetation at the edge of the common. Cross the stream to take a path descending to the right through the bracken. Below you is the deep valley of **Gogbatch**. Continue along its rim to eventually reach a house and then an open area of grassland.

❹ Across the grass here is another tarmacked lane. Cross to it, turn right, keep right at a junction, and continue to the bottom of the hill. Here turn right on a road descending to cross the stream and then running along the bottom of the valley. Where this road rises and bends right, opposite a house, a fingerpost marked **'Plush Hill'** points right.

❺ Follow this path up the hillside, go either way at the fork because the paths soon join again, and bend left to a path junction with a post. Turn left here on a path descending gently across open land. At the split on its far side, take the path bending left alongside the fence to arrive at a gate beside a house.

Shropshire Pub Walks

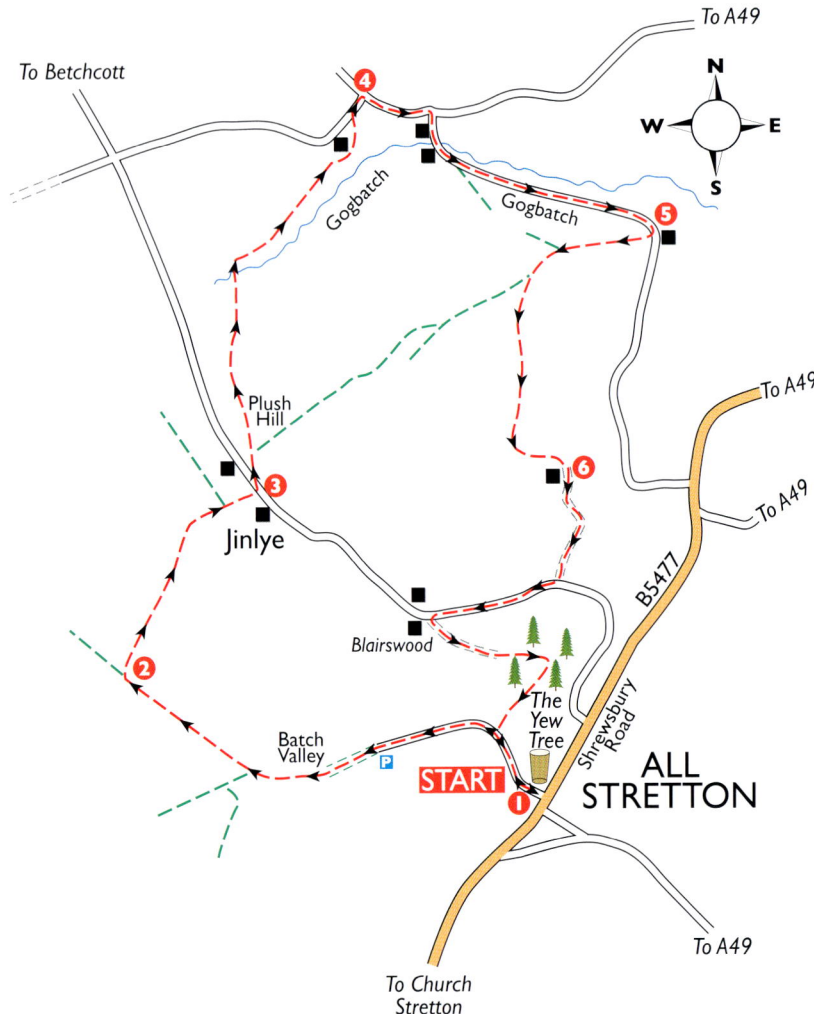

6 Continue ahead on the gravelled track, passing more houses, until in about 400 metres you reach a road. Turn right and climb quite steeply for some 300 metres. In front of the house called **Blairswood Cottage**, turn left on to a wide descending track passing other houses. Ultimately the track becomes a narrow high-banked path diving into woodland. A steep descent on a soft-underfoot woodland path follows, until after about 300

All Stretton 16

metres, you emerge on a road beside houses. This is **Batch Valley road** – simply turn left to return to the Yew Tree, or right to return to the valley car parks.

Place of Interest Nearby

If you have an appetite for more of the Long Mynd, just go a couple of miles down the road to Church Stretton. Here you can turn up the road to **Cardingmill Valley**, a lovely spot for a family picnic beside the stream. There's also a justly popular National Trust owned teashop/restaurant, and, of course, more walks up the hillsides. If that's not for you, or if it should be raining, go down into the town itself, where among the tearooms and many individual shops, the huge antiques emporium could possibly be the greatest attraction. Sat Nav SY6 6JG.

Walk 17
CLUN

Distance: 6 miles (9.8 km)

Start: The White Horse Inn, The Square, Clun, SY7 8JA.

Parking: The White Horse Inn does not have its own parking but roadside parking is usually possible. Beyond that, there is a small car park by the packhorse bridge (B4368 off Church Street) and ample parking at the Memorial Hall at Point 2 on this walk. Sat Nav SY7 8NY.

Map: OS Explorer 201 Knighton & Presteigne.
Grid Ref: SO301808.

Terrain: Field and woodland paths. Several stiles and many fields of grazing livestock.

Clun is surely about as far off the beaten track as you can get in Shropshire. Don't leave without taking a look at its 15th-century packhorse bridge over the River Clun and the ruined castle on its hillock behind. And since fascinating shops and eateries line its main street, you may find it quite difficult to get started on

Clun 17

this walk! When you do, though, you have here a circuit of the Clun Valley that passes through the rich woodland and lovely remote farmland on its flanks. The initial climb reaches a hidden dale whose tiny stream is then followed down to the hamlet of Clunton where it joins the river. The return is a wide track along the lower edge of handsome Sowdley Wood, always with glimpses of the Clun valley through the trees. It's a good length ramble that should leave you with an appetite for the hearty fare at the White Horse Inn.

THE PUB — **THE WHITE HORSE INN** at Clun is a classic village pub that feels unchanged by time. Step through the door and you are in a cosy bar with log fire, horse brasses, and low black beams, with rooms leading off on all sides – a small flag-floored dining room, a billiard room, another dining area where ceiling hooks suggest it might once have been a butcher's, and up a narrow back passageway, a tiny beer garden. There's a good menu, with most food sourced in Shropshire, while some of the beers and ales are produced even more locally in their own microbrewery. Go for Solar, Green Man or Loophole and you are in for a treat!

🌐 whitehorseclun.com   ☎ 01588 640305.

The Walk

1 From the **White Horse Inn**, walk east along the main street, passing the **Sun Inn**, and turn left where signed to the **Memorial Hall**. Turn right at the T-junction, bear left, and soon the **Memorial Hall** with its large car park is on your left.

2 Continue up the road, pass the **Youth Hostel**, and some 200 metres beyond, find a stile in the hedge on the right. Cross the corner of the field to another stile, and continue diagonally right to a stile accessing a hedged track. Turn right and climb on this

Shropshire Pub Walks

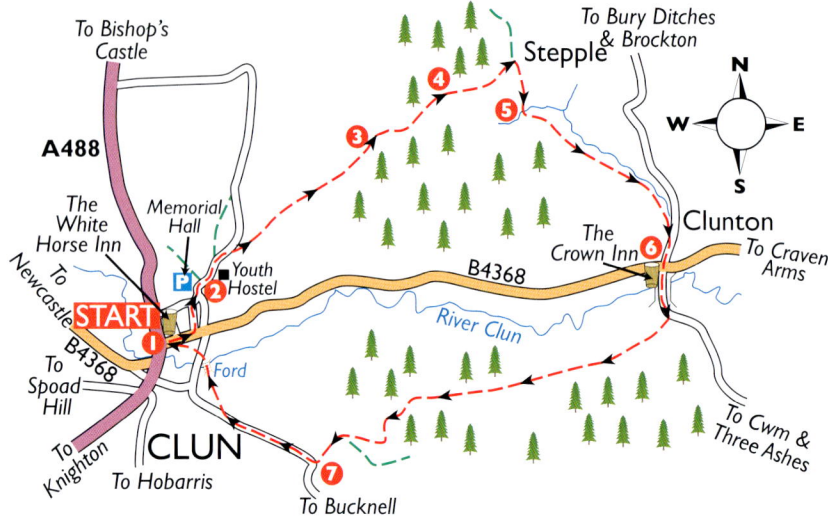

track, continuing after a gate, alongside the hedge in a field. The track maintains direction until, just over the brow of the hill, it reaches a gate into woodland.

❸ In the woods an obvious path bears right. Where the path splits go left, skirting the edge of the wood and descending quite steeply to a gate into a field. Turn right, keeping to the edge of the field to reach a metal gate. The path now bears diagonally right, crossing the stream on a plank bridge, and climbs to a broad track beside a wooden gate.

❹ Bear right on the track and continue to a metal gate in front of the farm buildings at **Stepple**. Keep ahead between buildings, then turn right where signed, on a descending track. A few metres after this track swings left, a gate on the right gives access to a field. Cross the field directly to descend to a gate before the stream at the bottom, and go through a second gate.

❺ Turn left and follow a path that looks like a sheepwalk through successive fields, with the stream always just to your left. After meeting a wider track, pass through two gates but do not cross the stream. The path continues alongside the stream, over a stile

Clun 17

and a gate, to reach a field with a farm track crossing. Keep ahead over this track to a stile in the hedge and a lane beyond. Turn right now to reach the main road in the village of **Clunton**.

6 Cross to the road opposite (**SP Clunton Coppice**). The **Crown Inn** stands on the corner and you may be able to refuel for the return journey! Continue up the road, crossing the **River Clun**, and where it begins to climb, go through a gate behind a lovely half-timbered house on the right. This rough track initially climbs abruptly between high banks, but then levels to follow the contours along the lower woodland edge for almost 2 miles. Emerging from the trees, keep ahead to meet a road at a bend.

7 Go right, continue past the junction, and with the road descending, look for a stile in the hedge on your right. Beyond this a field path takes you down to cross a plank bridge and then a footbridge over the **River Clun**, beside the ford. At the picnic area, keep ahead up the track which bends left and narrows to come out on the main road in **Clun**. The **White Horse Inn** is to your left here, the **Memorial Hall** to your right.

Place of Interest Nearby

If you return to Clunton and turn left, in a couple of miles you will arrive at the free parking area for **Bury Ditches**. The banks of this remarkable Iron Age hillfort were once covered by pine forest and were only revealed in 1978 when a storm blew down the trees. Huge ramparts ring the summit, where an orientation table names all the hills on a distant horizon. Sat Nav SY7 8BD.
🌐 forestryengland.uk/bury-ditches

Walk 18
Aston Munslow

Distance: 5½ miles (8.8 km)

Start: The Swan Inn, B4368, Aston Munslow, SY7 9ER

Parking: There is a large community (free) car park opposite The Swan Inn.

Map: OS Explorer 217 The Long Mynd & Wenlock Edge.
Grid Ref: SO512866.

Terrain: Field paths and quiet lanes.

Here you are in Corvedale, a place where many streams twist and wind their way from the relative heights of Wenlock Edge to form the River Corfe itself, en route for Ludlow and the Teme. Watched over by Shropshire's highest hill, Brown Clee, this is a valley of villages where time has stood still, where old stone or half-timbered cottages tucked away in overflowing gardens offer eggs or honey for sale at their gates. Diddlebury, with a stream at its heart, is possibly the gem of this walk – but then there are

Aston Munslow 18

lanes whose banks are bursting with wild flowers, and from the highest gorse-clad fields, views across the valley to the summit of distant Titterstone Clee. You'll probably want to return to Corvedale!

THE PUB **THE SWAN INN** dates back to the 14th century when it became an early coaching inn. The story goes that the young Dick Turpin once spent a night here – although given the much-romanticised highwayman's true list of crimes, that may not be much to brag about! But The Swan Inn reflects its age handsomely, its leaning walls, sagging roof timbers and rolling floors all sympathetically exuding character, and contributing to the welcoming atmosphere. The menu is extensive, and the locally-sourced food is as excellent as you might expect, with Shropshire ales on tap. With a lovely beer garden for summer and blazing log-fires for winter, The Swan is both friendly and dog-friendly. If you're a pub aficionado, then you certainly don't want to miss The Swan Inn!

🌐 theswaninnastonmunslow.co.uk ☎ 01584 841415.

The Walk

❶ From the parking area opposite the **Swan Inn** walk uphill into the village. At 'five-ways junction', turn sharp left, and in about 50 metres, go right on a gravelled track as signed. To the left of the last house, a track runs up to a stile into a field. Three more fields are crossed in quick succession before two stiles take you across a sunken track.

❷ Cross the next field directly, then in the last field, keep the hedge on your left to finally emerge on a narrow high-banked lane. Turn left, and follow it down to the road on the edge of **Diddlebury**.

❸ Cross the road, turn right on the pavement, and soon after crossing the end of **Mill Lane**, take a no through road on the right, signed to **Pinstones**. The lane climbs gently for something

Shropshire Pub Walks

like a mile, the view behind extending as you go. Eventually you pass through the farm of **Pinstones** and reach a track junction.

❹ Go sharp left here, through a metal gate into a field where there are solar panels. Continue with the hedge on your left until at the end of a line of gorse bushes, a broad grassy track doubles back downhill. A sharp left in front of a house takes you onto a track that soon descends through a wide grassy valley. Go through a gate at its far end to a track and then another tarmacked lane, which soon brings you back to the main road, beside the **Sun Inn**.

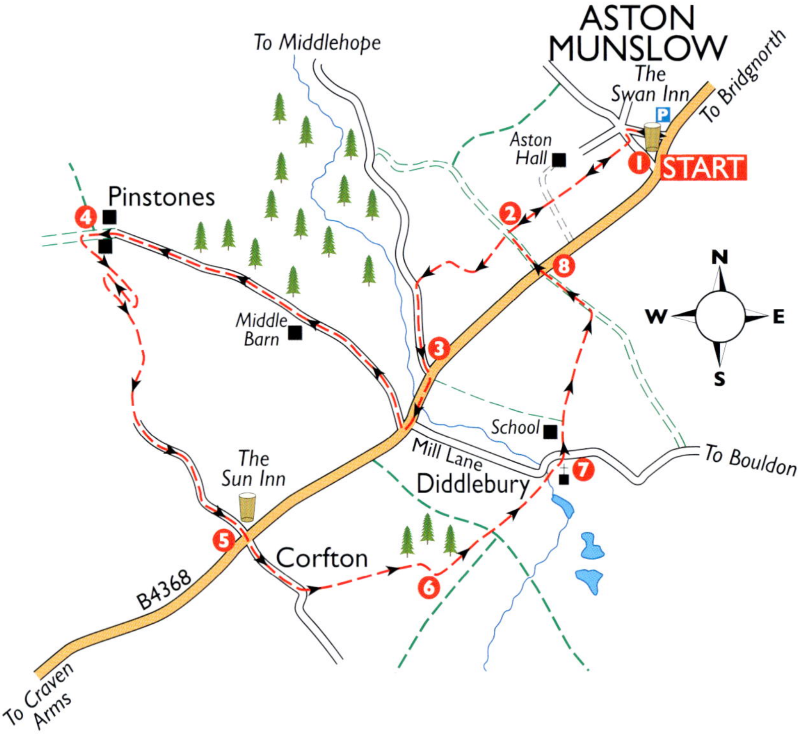

Aston Munslow 18

5 Cross to the road opposite and continue into **Lower Corfton**. With a large brick house in front of you, bear left to a kissing gate into a field. Cross this diagonally as directed by the arrow to another gate and stile giving onto a broad farm track. The path now heads diagonally across the field opposite to its top right-hand corner. Here a gap in the hedge leads to a signed kissing gate at the corner of a wood.

6 Keep alongside the woodland edge, then continue in the same direction across the large field, aiming just right of **Diddlebury church**. Here a kissing gate allows you to descend the field and turn left into the village. Cross the second footbridge (the one with the white rail) over the stream and walk up to the church.

7 Across the road now is the village hall. Stay right of the hall to find a kissing gate and enter a field. Now keep straight ahead with the school field on your left, and head for the bottom left corner of the field where there is a gate. Over the track, the next field is crossed directly to a stile leading onto a hedged bridleway. Turn left here to reach the main road.

8 Opposite you at this point is a very narrow and sometimes rather overgrown track between high hedges. Keep to this for about 150 metres to the place where you crossed it earlier (Point 2). Turn right and retrace your steps across the fields to **Aston Munslow**.

Place of Interest Nearby

Down the road in **Craven Arms**, the **Shropshire Hills Discovery Centre** can tell you everything you ever wanted to know about the area. The exhibition at the Centre offers a panoramic film that takes you floating high above the landscape, seemingly in a hot air balloon, while there's a good look at life in the county's many Iron Age hillforts, not to mention a replica skeleton of the woolly mammoth found in nearby Condover. A shop sells everything from walking guides to local artwork, appealing footpaths wander through adjacent Onny Meadows, and a café offers locally-sourced affordable meals. Grass-roofed and curved in mock-hillfort style, the Discovery Centre is more than worth a visit. Sat Nav SY7 9RS. ⊕ shropshirehillsdiscoverycentre.co.uk

Walk 19
LUDLOW

Distance: 6 miles (9.7 km)

Start: Castle Street Car Park, Castle Street, Ludlow, SY8 1AT.

Parking: The Rose and Crown has no parking. Castle Street Car Park (fee-paying) is off the market square, a couple of minutes' walk from the pub. You might also consider the limited (4 hours) free roadside parking near Dinham Bridge, passed at the end of the walk.

Map: OS Explorer 203 Ludlow. **Grid Ref:** SO510746.

Terrain: Easy field paths and quiet lanes. No stiles. Dog-friendly.

'Probably the loveliest town in England' was John Betjeman's pronouncement on Ludlow, and with that in mind, you know that just walking around the town will be a real pleasure. Fine Georgian houses line streets leading down to the River Teme, while a 12th-century castle overlooks the tumbling waters;

Ludlow 19

narrow alleyways harbour independent shops, and a lively market fills the town square most days of the week.

Hard as it will be to tear yourself away, this easy walk takes you to another interesting place, the village of Bromfield. Here you will pass the Ludlow Food Centre, an establishment showcasing locally produced food of all kinds. Maybe you won't want to fill your rucksack with apples, but perhaps a small meat pie or two? When you've settled that question, there's a fine old church, a gateway to a priory, a ruined mill, and some lovely parkland for the way home.

THE PUB

THE ROSE AND CROWN on Church Street is Ludlow's oldest pub, ale having been served on the site since the 13th century. Situated in its own concealed courtyard in the centre of town, the pub has recently been restored in keeping with its antiquity, its interior divided into nooks and crannies, rooms and alcoves. Wood is everywhere, from floors to beams, pew seats to oak panelling – and you can entertain yourself before your meal by searching for wood carvings of seven mice and a beaver by Robert 'Mouseman' Thompson. Dogs are welcome inside but there is also outside seating in two courtyards well-decked with flowers in summer.

The Rose and Crown is a Joule's pub, with their Slumbering Monk beer being very popular. Food is fairly standard pub fare, but the pork pies have something of a reputation, 'large' being just that! ⊕ joulesbrewery.co.uk/our-taphouses/our-pub-list/rose-and-crown-ludlow
☎ 01584 875726.

The Walk

❶ From the car park turn right towards the castle and then go right around its walls. The path splits at a big beech tree. Turn sharp right here, walk down to the road, and keep left, descending again. Continue now on the pavement alongside this road until it corners right.

Shropshire Pub Walks

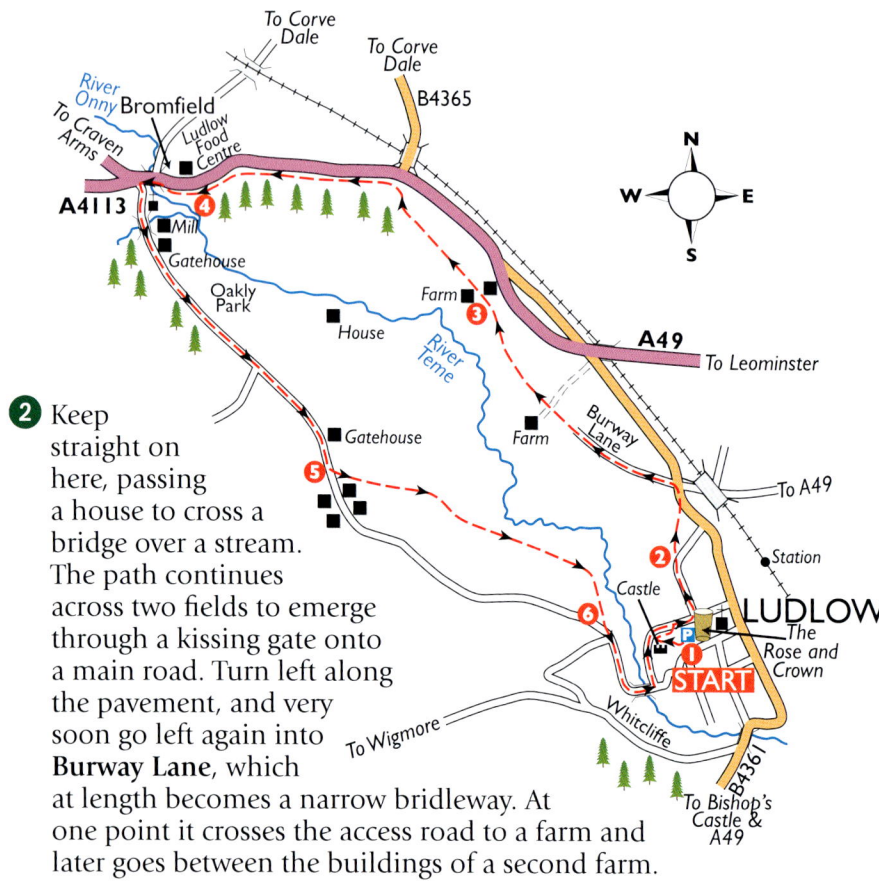

2 Keep straight on here, passing a house to cross a bridge over a stream. The path continues across two fields to emerge through a kissing gate onto a main road. Turn left along the pavement, and very soon go left again into **Burway Lane**, which at length becomes a narrow bridleway. At one point it crosses the access road to a farm and later goes between the buildings of a second farm.

3 Simply keep ahead as signed through the farm, going through a small field to emerge in very large field. The bridleway then runs along its whole length on the left-hand edge, finally bending right beside woodland. Just before reaching the road, turn left with the bridleway to continue between trees alongside the road for almost a mile to its end in **Bromfield**.

> *At this point the Ludlow Food Centre and its adjacent café are almost opposite, but you will need to cross a fairly busy road to visit them.*

4 Back with the road on your right again, cross the bridge over the **River Onny** and immediately turn left to pass the **Church of St Mary the Virgin**.

Ludlow

A Grade I listed sandstone building, it was originally the church of a Benedictine Priory. The restored medieval gatehouse to that Priory stands just along the road.

Continue down the road to cross the stone bridge over the **River Teme**, with a ruined 19th-century corn mill to the left. The road now continues past a gatehouse into the grounds of **Oakly Park**, with just the occasional glimpse of the house itself across the fields. Continue on this quiet road, keeping ahead at a junction (**SP Ludlow**), until after about a mile you reach another gatehouse, and a path junction some 100 metres beyond.

5 Turn left on a path between hedges signed as the **Shrophire Way**, which you will now follow all the way back to **Ludlow**. The well-marked and well-trodden path soon bends right to cross two fields, then crosses a small stream to climb on the other side. After cutting the corner of another field, it then follows its left-hand edge for some 600 metres. Two more fields are crossed, all clearly signed, before the path arrives at a lane beside houses.

6 Turn left and keep ahead with some fine views of **Ludlow Castle** across the river. Pass the roadside parking and turn left to cross **Dinham Bridge**. On the far side, turn left, then bear right up a path climbing back up to the castle and the market square.

Place of Interest Nearby

Ludlow Castle dates from around 1100 and grew in importance when it became home to the Council of the Marches of Wales under Edward IV. Royalty were frequent visitors; Arthur; the older brother of Henry VIII died here, and Edward V, whose premature accession to the throne led to his disappearance in the Tower, spent his childhood here. Much of the castle is in ruins now, but there is still a lot to explore with accessible narrow walkways and spiral staircases to add to the experience. ludlowcastle.com

Walk 20
HOPTON WAFERS

Distance: 4½ miles (7.2 km)

Start: The Hopton Crown, Hopton Wafers, DY14 0NB.

Parking: The proprietor is happy for anyone to park at The Crown when it is not open (i.e. before 4pm Monday to Thursday). During opening hours, at least some custom (coffee, etc) might reasonably be expected.

Map: OS Explorer 203 Ludlow. **Grid Ref:** SO637762.

Terrain: Field paths and quiet lanes in rolling countryside. Many stiles.

In the early 1800s, the land around Hopton Wafers belonged to one Thomas Botfield, a Fellow of the Royal Society, magistrate, and deputy-lieutenant of Shropshire, with interests in geology, metallurgy, the arts, horticulture, and more. His home, the Georgian mansion Hopton Court, is passed at the end of this walk, although it can only be glimpsed through the trees, while his elaborate tomb stands prominently in the churchyard. Before you get there though, there's Ditton watermill with its ford, the

Hopton Wafers 20

Elan Valley pipeline, and splendid views from every hilltop ridge in this undulating off-the-beaten-track countryside.

THE PUB

THE HOPTON CROWN, once a 17th-century coaching inn, is today a fairly large establishment with several guest rooms. It nevertheless manages to exude a feeling of comfort and relaxation, no doubt enhanced by its low beams and enormous open fire. The two bars, old and new, are complemented by two dining rooms, one of which is dog-friendly – and even the four-footed can enjoy the luxury of a carpet! An alternative of outdoor seating is possible on fine days. The menu is wide and the food of high quality, with local Shropshire beers to accompany and an excellent wine list. Restricted opening hours so check website before visiting. ⊕ hoptoncrown.co.uk ☎ 01299 887101.

The Walk

❶ From the pub car park turn right for about 20 metres, and cross the road to an unsigned track alongside a house. Pass a bungalow to go through a gate to a track between trees. After a stile the tree-lined track carries on to emerge in a field. Continue alongside the hedge almost to its end, where a gate on the left admits you to another field. Now walk downhill, bearing slightly left, to find a footbridge hidden in trees.

❷ Maintain your direction across the next field to a stile opposite. In this next field, which may be rather overgrown, the **Elan Valley pipeline** lies in an obvious ditch.
  The Elan Valley pipeline carries water from the Elan reservoir in mid-Wales to Birmingham entirely by gravity, a distance of 73 miles, taking 1½ days.
Keep right along the hedge in this field to pick up a track flanked by wooden fencing, eventually descending to a **Chalet Park**.

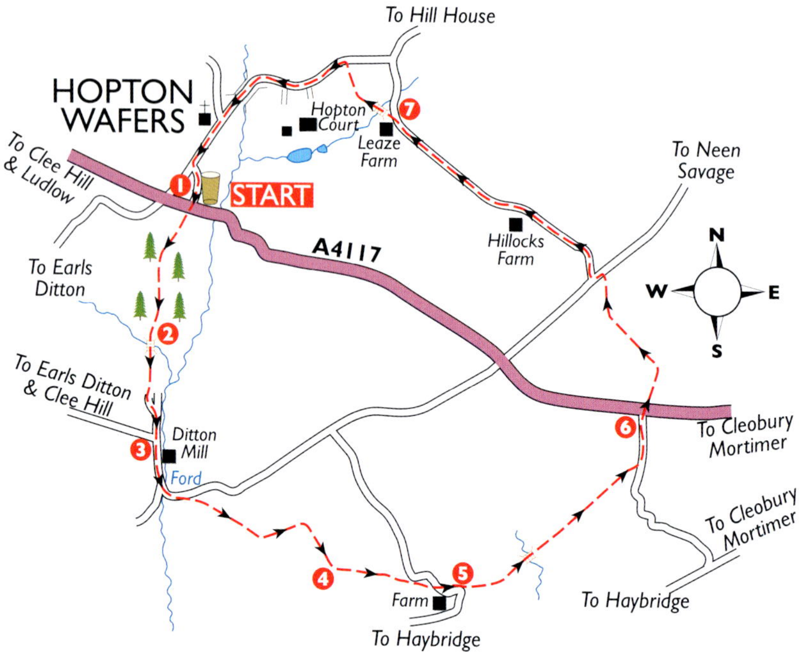

Shropshire Pub Walks

Follow the road ahead to a T-junction and turn right to reach a public road.

❸ Turn left, downhill, to pass **Ditton Mill** and continue across the ford to climb on its far side. Where the road corners left, climb steps on the right to cross a stile into a field. The path now continues along the right-hand edge of this large field, until shortly after passing a pond, a gate is reached. Go through, and still with the hedge on your right, climb to the summit of the ridge.

❹ Cross a track to a stile opposite and aim diagonally left across the field as shown by the arrow. Reaching the far side, turn right and continue with the hedge on your left, past a gate, to reach a stile before a farm. The road ahead now passes farm

Hopton Wafers 20

buildings and a lovely half-timbered farmhouse to a corner with a stile on the left.

5 In this field, the path hugs the right-hand edge for maybe 150 metres, then bears left across the field to a ditch at the bottom. Here a footbridge carries you across to climb straight up the field on the far side. Cross a stile, maintaining your direction to cross another stile, then turn right to cross yet another. In the final field bear diagonally left towards a wooden building in the far corner and descend to a lane. Turn left to join the main road.

6 Cross to take the track diagonally right. This soon passes through the hedge and continues round bends and through gates to emerge on a lane. Turn left for about 30 metres, then at the junction, right. Follow this quiet lane past **Hillocks Farm** and down to **Leaze Farm**, a distance of about ⅔ mile.

7 Where the road bends right, go through a gate ahead to cross a footbridge over a stream. On the far side, go diagonally right to a gate at the top field corner, then cross a larger field to big metal gates opening onto a lane. Turn left and follow this lane past two entrances to **Hopton Court**.

As you descend the hill, look for Thomas Botfield's 'Chair', a stone seat on the edge of woodland on your right. Coming into Hopton Wafers, you pass St Michael's Church, which was endowed by Thomas Botfield. His memorial stands in front of it.

Continue to the road junction and turn left to return to the **Hopton Crown**.

Place of Interest Nearby

Two miles west of Hopton Wafers, the road climbs **Clee Hill**. It's not the highest of Shropshire's summits but there's a splendid roadside viewpoint from where, on a clear day, you can pick out the Malverns, Black Mountains and Brecon Beacons. Sporting the masts and domes of an air traffic control centre along with evidence of long-past mining activity, the actual summit of Clee Hill has even better views. And if climbing's not your thing, no matter – there's a road that takes you all the way.

OTHER TITLES FROM COUNTRYSIDE BOOKS

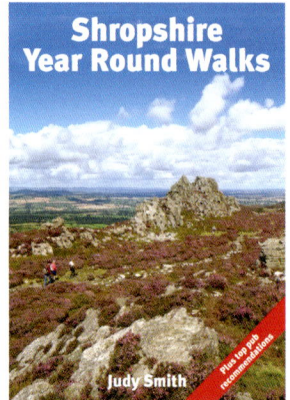
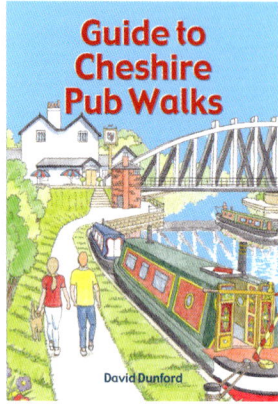
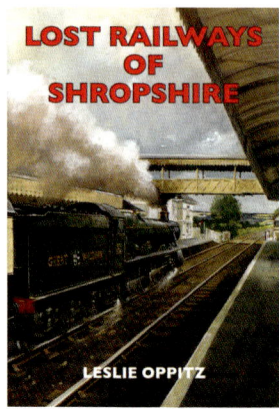
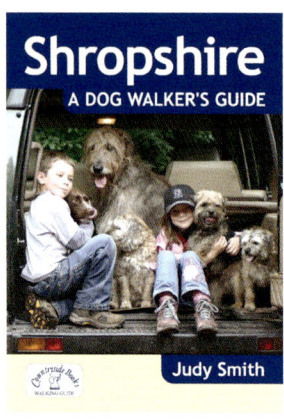

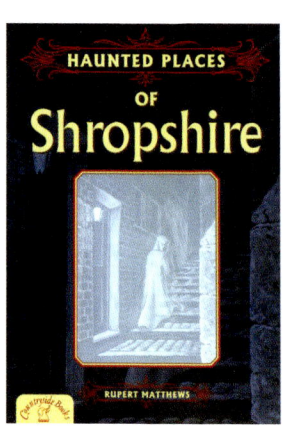
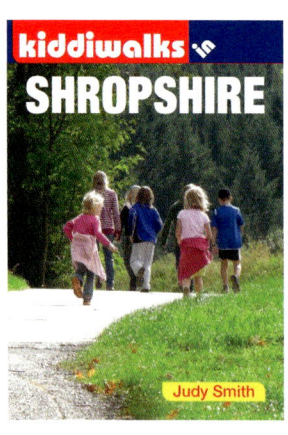
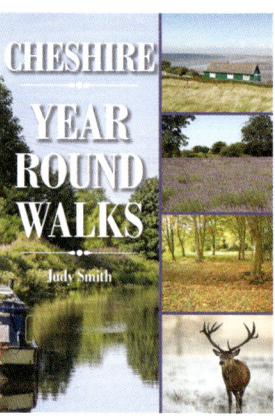
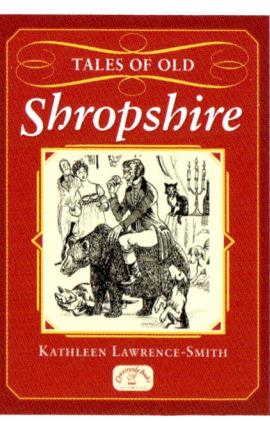

To see the full range of books by Countryside Books please visit
www.countrysidebooks.co.uk

Follow us on @CountrysideBooks